# Developing Cross-Cultural Competence for Leaders

This book offers an accessible reference and roadmap for the practical application of cross-cultural competence (3C) for leaders dedicated to leading with diversity, inclusion and personal development in mind.

*Developing Cross-Cultural Competence for Leaders* takes readers from ideational to real, asking them to step out of their comfort zone and learn to navigate cultural differences. The authors invite readers to join them on a journey of discovery of themselves, their personal and professional peers and ultimately the cultural landscape they inhabit both knowingly and oftentimes unknowingly all in the hopes of opening doors to empathetic and effective communication. The skillset required for 3C is developed throughout the book beginning with a discussion of relevant concepts, leading the readers through narratives of extreme environments and ending with a roadmap for use in leadership positions. Each chapter discusses a foundational idea contextualized with sample narratives and ending with thought questions. The authors summon readers to embrace dissimilarities, shift perspectives, dare to engage and navigate in new and even adverse social and cultural contexts.

*Developing Cross-Cultural Competence for Leaders* is an essential reading for students of leadership development, as well as military and non-military professionals.

**Joseph J. Thomas** is Director of The Stockdale Center for Ethical Leadership at the United States Naval Academy in Annapolis, Maryland.
**Clementine K. Fujimura** is a Cultural Anthropologist and Professor at the United States Naval Academy in Annapolis, Maryland.

JOSEPH J. THOMAS AND
CLEMENTINE K. FUJIMURA

# Developing
# Cross-Cultural
# Competence for
# Leaders
## A Guide

Routledge
Taylor & Francis Group

NEW YORK AND LONDON

Cover image: © Getty images

First published 2022
by Routledge
605 Third Avenue, New York, NY 10158

and by Routledge
4 Park Square, Milton Park, Abingdon, Oxon, OX14 4RN

Routledge is an imprint of the Taylor & Francis Group, an informa business

Library of Congress Cataloging-in-Publication Data
A catalog record for this title has been requested

ISBN: 978-1-032-10044-9 (hbk)
ISBN: 978-1-032-10043-2 (pbk)
ISBN: 978-1-003-21335-2 (ebk)

DOI: 10.4324/9781003213352

Typeset in Joanna MT
by Apex CoVantage, LLC

# Contents

Leadership matters. Leadership is especially challenging when it involves people from diverse cultural backgrounds. In decades of researching and leading global health initiatives and peacekeeping and stabilization operations, I have seen, analyzed and written about how carefully planned operations can go seriously awry because of a lack of cultural understanding. In some of the instances upon which I reported it was a lack of understanding of the different organizational cultures involved in a project. In others, it was a lack of understanding of the local cultures where the initiatives were taking place. And, in yet others, it was because of a combination of misapprehensions due to both misunderstanding the actions of local actors and misunderstanding the actions of colleagues from other agencies.

For the most part those who have taken on leadership challenges in multicultural environments have had two distinct places to which they could turn for advice. There are, first, a myriad of books and articles about the dynamics of leadership. Second, there is an abundant literature advising how better to work across cultures. Only rarely are the two streams of work brought together. In *Developing Cross-Cultural Competence for Leaders*, Drs. Thomas and Fujimura begin to fill this gap, and they do so with a notable combination of theoretical sophistication, broad experience in leading and teaching about leadership in cross-cultural settings, and by giving practical advice for how to develop the skills and orientations necessary for effective culturally aware leadership.

Thomas and Fujimura are exceptionally well-suited as guides to the exploration of cross-culturally competent leadership. Together they bring decades of experience leading complex organizations and in teaching about leadership through a cross-cultural lens. That their individual experiences come from distinct organizational perspectives—military leadership and academic administration and anthropological research—brings added depth to the conversation that their book develops.

Too often instruction on working cross-culturally stops at the level of what I have characterized as "Travelers Advice," focusing on lists of "facts" about how other cultures deal with the world and offering a basic list of things a person engaging members of other groups should or should not do. *Developing Cross-Cultural Competence for Leaders* goes well beyond this and introduces its readers to more sophisticated understandings of culture.

Thomas's and Fujimura's emphasis on treating culture as a source for helping people create meaning from their experiences necessarily leads them to discuss culture with greater nuance. Adopting the idea that culture has representational, directive and affective force provides a platform for discussing a variety of complex issues about culture, and they do that in ways that are at once sophisticated and accessible to the reader. As one progresses through *Developing Cross-Cultural Competence for Leaders* they gain an increasingly refined understanding of how culture affects leadership and how they can become sensitized to the complexities that entails. Several of the themes they develop in this book rate being noted here.

Thomas and Fujimura emphasize the importance of experiential learning in developing cross-cultural competencies. I especially appreciate that they acknowledge that mere exposure to other cultures is not sufficient for developing an appreciation for cultural difference. Indeed, such unguided encounters, or encounters that don't include constructive reflection can have the opposite effect, confirming one's ethnocentric biases. So, one of the most welcome features of this book is the very practical, structured and doable reflexive exercises that Thomas and Fujimura present. The suggestions they offer for systematic structuring of cross-cultural training, all of which they have worked out over decades of training emerging leaders, are straightforward, useful and offer clear lessons for leaders.

I appreciate too that in developing their discussions the authors recognize that culture does not reside just in the way people think about their environments and experiences. Rather, Thomas and Fujimura show us that culture is also felt—it is embodied—in, as we might say, "the gut." They appropriately warn against acting on our "gut reactions" to cultures other than our own because doing so can lead to a number of errors in thinking when they engage the heuristics and biases to which our thinking can fall prey. Thomas and Fujimura suggest that such reactions be avoided by subjecting experience to structured reflection, and they offer tools to make that reflection productive. The view of culture that Thomas and Fujimura adopt also makes it plain that culture orients peoples actions, but it does not determine them, and that as a result culture is dynamic and changing. The tools that Thomas and Fujimura present in this book give us the ability to figure out the cultural components of troubling interactions and to address those in productive ways.

Although they review approaches to cross-cultural understanding and leadership that draw on a dimensional analysis of culture, Thomas and Fujimura go well beyond those analyses. Their focus on culture as a meaning system leads them to revealing discussions about how things that appear familiar, including social relations and the words we use to describe situations, may well have different meanings for those from cultures other than our own. Reading *Developing Cross-Cultural Competence for Leaders* reminded me of how efforts at civil–military coordination during the early 1990s interventions in Somalia foundered because the international civil servants, military and nongovernmental organization participants in those efforts brought to their discussions different organizational culture-base understandings of the shared term "security."

In engaging such issues, Thomas and Fujimura move the reader's focus from the surface traveler's advice to looking at the underlying cultural logics that people use. It is refreshing to see their focus on the cultural why in addition to the what, something that is often absent from cross-cultural training materials. They make clear that because scope matters cultural understandings shift in relation to the challenges at hand, and that thus developing cultural competencies is a process not an endpoint.

*Developing Cross-Cultural Competence for Leaders* is unique in the sophistication with which it combines theoretical discussions, advice for training and clear lessons for leaders. The need for active, careful, reflexive engagement when addressing cross-cultural questions resonates throughout the book. Investment in, the study of, and the implementation of the advice offered by Drs. Thomas and Fujimura will pay dividends throughout a leader's career.

Robert A. Rubinstein, Ph.D., MsPH
Distinguished Professor of Anthropology
Professor of International Relations
The Maxwell School of Syracuse University

*Developing Cross-Cultural Competence for Leaders*

JOSEPH J. THOMAS AND CLEMENTINE K. FUJIMURA

## WHY THIS BOOK—AND WHY NOW

The time for leaders to develop cross-cultural competence (3C), which involves constructive communication skills across cultural contexts on an off-line and across organizations and government institutions, is now. As evidenced by global leaders, especially in times of tension, there are situations and problems that require cultural understanding. Throughout the world, interpersonal and cultural differences are pronounced due to diversification of systems of communication (social and online networks, for example), virtual engagement, cultural variation within businesses and governments and management styles and linguistic differences—including dialects and idioms within languages that are often shaped by social stratification and heritage. As we reflect on the past years, on the social movements and often violent social upheavals, we realize that differences prevail and that leaders seeking to mitigate strife have not achieved 3C: Many have failed in acquiring the ability to truly understand the perspective of others. Many have not realized the importance of doing so and have ultimately failed in their ability to negotiate differences effectively. This book offers a path for individuals to improve their ability at perspective-taking and effective communication.

Given that cross-cultural competence (3C) is the ingredient that is often absent in interpersonal and interagency communication today, this book highlights foundational theories and challenges leaders to engage in a committed effort to develop 3C knowledge, skills and aptitudes. The authors, Joe Thomas, a retired Marine and director of The Stockdale Center for Ethical Leadership, and Clementine Fujimura, a cultural anthropologist at the United States Naval Academy, take readers from ideational to real, asking them to step out of their comfort zones and to learn to navigate cultural differences. The authors invite readers

1  **Introduction**

DOI: 10.4324/9781003213352-1

to engage in a journey of self-discovery, to probe the perspectives of their personal and professional peers, and ultimately explore the cultural landscape they inhabit—both knowingly and oftentimes unknowingly—all in the hopes of opening doors to empathetic and effective communication. The skill set required for 3C is developed throughout the book, beginning with a discussion of relevant concepts, followed by an examination of narratives of unfamiliar environments, with each chapter ending with questions and exercises for use by those in or aspiring to be in leadership positions. The authors summon readers to embrace dissimilarities, shift perspectives, dare to engage, and navigate within new and even adverse social and cultural contexts.

### BOOK OVERVIEW

This book offers a reference for practical application of cross-cultural competence for leaders. It is not meant to be exhaustive in its presentation of theory, but rather it is designed to be accessible for everyone who is dedicated to leading with diversity, inclusion and personal development in mind. Each chapter discusses a foundational idea, contextualized with sample narratives and ending with thought questions. These thought questions reflect the basic premise of this handbook: Without practice, without the experience of using and experimenting with ideas first encountered in reading, lectures, or otherwise, true assimilation of the ideas—that is, true learning—cannot take place.

Chapter 1: Defining Culture for Leadership

Chapter 1 offers a definition of the concept most fundamental to cross-cultural competence, that of culture. Each individual you meet is the embodiment of a unique intersection of cultural experiences that a person has gained throughout their lifetime. This cultural persona cannot be the exact same as your own since each individual's experiences are unique. This chapter explores the complexity of culture and of individuals as cultural beings and takes into account the history, within scholarly writing, of attempts at giving a single definition to culture. The author offers contextualizing narratives from Japan, Russia and the United States, in both higher education and business settings. The purpose of this chapter is to allow readers to gain a sense of themselves and the people they encounter as cultural beings. Through the use of thought questions, the chapter offers the reader ideas on how to grasp and make use of the culture concept, personally and professionally. The chapter will help readers gain appreciation for other peoples' perspectives and to recognize and consider the wealth of experience that has caused people to reflect on, and respond to, situations in different ways—whether the situations be of global proportion or within a particular work or personal space.

### Chapter 2: Cross-Cultural Understanding as a Function of Leadership

Chapter 2 investigates the intersection of culture and leadership on a variety of levels. It is well known that a leader must align and work to support an organization's core values and understand the beliefs and desired behaviors to enable effective outcomes. A strong leader will, among other things, reinforce the ideals of the organization. Beyond embracing the organization's ideals, a leader must also understand its membership culture(s) and leadership culture. The intersection of all of the possible subcultures in an organization can be leveraged to facilitate the mission. This chapter explores the key areas in which the intersection of leadership and culture is paramount to achieve success via a discussion of significant theories presented such as the GLOBE study, Hofstede's Cultural Dimensions Theory and others. A summary of takeaways for leaders in developing 3C as well as a cultural awareness self-assessment are offered in conclusion to this rich exploration of concepts, ideas and social scientific studies.

### Chapter 3: Experiential Learning and Immersive Environments to Develop Leaders

Experiential learning has deep roots in academia. The chapter begins with a grounding in a sampling of theoretical frameworks common to any learning environment. For applied skills such as leadership and cross-cultural competence (3C), participating in a complementary field experience is critically important. Linking the two elements of leader development can be difficult, time-consuming work. Nowhere, however, does this investment pay such immediate and lasting dividends as in international travel. Directly experiencing subtle differences in communication, decision-making and style between different cultures can be a life-altering experience—but only if prepared for appropriately. It is also just as important to effectively explore lessons learned *after* the immersive experience. By employing practical suggestions for getting the most of cross-cultural experiences, this chapter will help the reader to engage best practices in experiential learning.

### Chapter 4: The Ethnographic Method for Leadership

This chapter delves into experiential learning by offering the method of ethnography to help guide leaders through cross-cultural terrain. While traditionally a method of study used by scholars of anthropology, ethnography can be useful for lay people in everyday encounters. Ethnographic practice forces a person to develop cultural situational awareness through systematic yet flexible engagement and reflection. Of significance is the role of sensitive and meaningful intercultural communication, a skill that begs continuous practice and refining. This chapter also addresses methods for sharpening the reader's intercultural communication skills, through narrative examples and questions for thought as well as personal and practical application.

### Chapter 5: Developing 3C in the Workplace and the Role of Communication

Cross-cultural competence depends on the effort a person takes to continuously develop understanding, skills and curiosity in new contexts. This chapter explores opportunities for 3C development, as well as the necessity of enhancing communication skills. Opportunities can be found in surrounding communities, including the workplace, nearby campuses and other accessible institutions. It is hoped that via this chapter, readers will step out of their comfort zone to search and interact with new and various communities other than their own. Once again the authors encourage practicing, engaging, reflecting and learning from experiences. These experiences require effort but will enhance leaders not only professionally but most likely personally as well. When you gain the ability to communicate effectively across these communities, the skills and aptitudes required for adaptability and leadership success will develop and that implies that 3C will flourish.

### Chapter 6: Biases and Obstacles to Critical Thinking

This chapter calls for the reader to uncover hidden biases that impede the development of cross-cultural competence. We begin with a discussion of heuristics: the mental shortcuts in decision-making that allow complex problems to be solved quickly and efficiently. These shortcuts serve as quick mental references as we make judgments about the world around us—shortcuts that help us conserve time and mental energy. When navigating unfamiliar environments, however, we often employ heuristics that do not translate effectively to the new environment. Employing such systematic patterns in decision-making without accounting for the novel demands of a new environment becomes an obstacle to critical thinking. These deviations from rational judgment are commonly referred to as biases—or more specifically, cognitive biases. This chapter examines the nature and types of cognitive biases that prevent us from effectively engaging with unfamiliar cultures and it offers practical advice for better awareness and prevention of biased thinking.

### Chapter 7: Optimizing 3C with Key Ingredients: Empathy, Mindfulness and Reflexivity

This chapter emphasizes the importance of continuous self-development and investigation into one's own persona in working towards cross-cultural competence. It exposes often confounded terms of sympathy and empathy, the significance of empathy and its corollaries: mindfulness and reflexivity. After an introduction to these aptitudes, the authors offer real-life experiences to explore the impact of these when utilized or mismanaged. Theories such as that of the interpersonal gap, what it means to be "in" and cultural salient concepts are brought to life via personal narratives. The bottom line of this chapter is that it is not until we use our knowledge and imagination to take the perspective of others, not until we understand that seemingly basic notions of family, time and space, for example, are perceived differently in different societies, that we can engage in deep, meaningful, respectful and supportive ways with people from different backgrounds.

### Conclusion: The Personal and Organizational Benefits of Being Cross-Culturally Competent

While an individual's knowledge, skills and abilities grow through cross-cultural immersion, the most significant benefit gained from cross-cultural competence is organizational effectiveness. Leaders who are cross-culturally competent foster cross-culturally competent teams that are more cohesive and effective at problems-solving—and they raise the performance level of every individual on the team. This chapter describes organizational benefits and outcomes associated with 3C.

## ABOUT THE AUTHORS

**Joseph J. Thomas** currently serves as director of the VADM James B. Stockdale Center for Ethical Leadership at the United States Naval Academy (USNA) in Annapolis, Maryland. A retired Marine, he served previously as the Class of 1961 Professor of Leadership Education at USNA and as director of the MajGen John A. Lejeune Leadership Institute at Marine Corps University in Quantico, Virginia. In addition, Thomas has taught at the University of Notre Dame, University of Maryland, George Washington University, and the National Outdoor Leadership School. He has published five books on the topics of leadership and ethics, along with numerous articles, book chapters, and research reports. Thomas supported student research that led to the award of Rhodes, Mitchell and Fulbright scholarships. He's also planned and led cultural immersion expeditions to South Africa, Tibet, Turkey, Vietnam, Morocco, Peru, Jordan, India and Mongolia and has taught at service academies and war colleges in Central Asia, Eastern Europe and throughout Africa. Thomas holds master's degrees from the Maxwell School of Citizenship and Public Affairs at Syracuse University and the U.S. Army War College, a Ph.D. from George Mason University and a Certificate in Public Leadership from the Brookings Institute.

About himself he writes:

In my first career as a U.S. Marine Corps officer, I had an opportunity to travel to and work across Asia, Europe, Africa and Australia. Much of that work involved developing personal as well as professional relationships with coalition partners from many nations. While I lived in Japan for several years, most of my work involved shorter duration engagements. At times I found myself on planning teams in multi-national environments lasting days or even weeks. Patterns of effective interaction began to emerge as I noticed the most experienced participants had certain qualities—they listened carefully, spoke clearly and seemed to understand what every unique situation and individual needed. They employed interpersonal relationship techniques that bridged cultural differences regardless of the nationality or cultural background of the assembled international teams. I found myself writing down my observations and building upon my own understanding and abilities. In short, I came to think of cross-cultural competence as a learned skill—not unlike other aspects of leadership such as communication and decision-making—and one of immense and growing importance in our increasingly interconnected world. Language skills were important, but there is far more to connecting effectively than mere language skills. Understanding specific cultural dynamics is similarly important, but even that is not the key. Adopting a broad, global understanding of ways to bridge cultural differences seems to be the most important skill of all. This skill is rooted in a mindset.

In my second career as a civilian faculty member at the U.S. Naval Academy, my international commitments have continued. I've had opportunities to teach at service academies and war colleges across Africa, Europe and Asia. As I became more aware of the relevance and importance of these experiences for the development of my Naval Academy students, I began to design immersive experiences that could offer a crash course in cross-cultural competence. Language, Regional Expertise and Culture (LREC) immersions sponsored by our International Programs Office offered a chance to study a culture for a semester or two and follow that with a direct, ground-level engagement with that culture. LRECs last around three weeks and are best experienced by planning deliberate interactions with nearly every aspect of culture—the food, social norms, work, language, entertainment, family life and even physical environment of our targeted culture. All of this is possible with proper planning. I also discovered that living among remote cultures in austere environments was the optimal way of learning. The more different the culture is to my American students' experience the better. The more physically, psychologically and emotionally uncomfortable I can make them, the better. Remote cultures, we have discovered, are cultures writ with a darker pen.

That many of these cultures happened to be minorities within larger cultural contexts helped us see how struggles between peoples could be understood and, ultimately, remedied. With each interaction we learned more about ourselves and our own cultural identity. We learned what was negotiable and non-negotiable. We discovered our newfound skills could be employed to bring about important change even as we became more comfortable with uncertainty, complexity and ambiguity. By traveling and living among the Quechua in Peru, we experienced how indigenous people can adapt language, social and religious practices to make them their own. From the Tuareg people of North Africa and Bedouin of Jordan we learned how meshing ancient and modern economic practices could result in a happy life—if not prosperous in a way Westerners measure prosperity. We learned how the Kurds retained their ancient cultural identity in the face of great pressure to change throughout much of the Middle East. In places like Tibet, Mongolia, Vietnam and Kashmiri India we lived, ate and traveled with people as they went about their daily lives. The so-called learning curve is steep, but well worth it.

It is for all these reasons and more this book includes not just observations of how to think about culture, but practical advice on how to develop the skill essential to thriving in our increasingly interconnected world—cross-cultural competence. With chapters on ethnography, experiential learning and bias awareness, we hope this book brings together all those things needed to be a savvy traveler and effective leader.

**Clementine K. Fujimura** is a cultural anthropologist, professor of Anthropology, Russian and German and the Director of Area Studies at the United States Naval Academy in Annapolis. Her early research focused on the welfare of marginalized youth groups in the United States and Russia, culminating in numerous articles and two books on the subject. More recently, to combat ageism, she has conducted ethnographic research involving aging populations. Fujimura has published extensively on cultural understanding of marginalized groups in Russia and the United States, as well as on cultural education in the military. Her research seeks to move leaders to consider diverse perspectives in order to foster the well-being of populations in the United States and around the world. She has published extensively on the subject of military culture as well as on the use of animals in human therapy. With developing cross-culturally competent leaders as her passion, she teaches Cultural and Military Anthropology, Intercultural Communication, Area Studies, Cyber-ethnography, Russian Language and German Literature and Film. She enjoys mentoring and coaching those in higher education and business in intercultural communication skills. In her spare time, Fujimura serves on a number of Boards including the Community Advisory Board for WYPR/NPR. She is also the proud mother of two sons, one currently serving as an officer in the United States Marine Corps and the younger as a midshipman at the United States Naval Academy.

About herself she writes:

I was born in the United States but spent my formative years in various countries in Europe including England, France, Germany and Russia. As a child I was quickly attuned to the fact that uniqueness among cultures and societies demanded that in order for me to form relationships and friendships I needed to heed the nuanced differences between individual micro cultures such as age, ethnic and other sub-culture groups. Without a sensitivity to the difference in outlooks and beliefs, as a continuous outsider at the time, I would end up without my own cohort group and ultimately not find my own communities. While the ability to adapt and engage effectively in diverse cultural contexts had no name for me at the time, it became a matter of inter-personal survival among peers. Children can be tough on each other sometimes!

As I entered the realm of higher education I tested my ability to become a part of a community by consciously deciding to behave the way I believed my peers found acceptable and likeable. For example, I refrained from certain mannerisms my family had espoused including directness since in some of my international peer groups, indirect-ness was valued. By consciously stepping out of my comfort zone and code-switching, I became more effective in developing interpersonal and ultimately professional relationships. My interest in 3C led me to new cultural contexts in which I was able to conduct ethnographic research including (but not limited to) homeless and orphaned chil-dren and youth in Russia, military subcultures such as the LGBTQ+ communities in the United States military, online support communi-ties and senior communities in nursing homes and independent living spaces. Continuously working on 3C personally has enriched my life as a scholar, teacher and leader. It is a passion I look forward to sharing with my students and readers.

Finally, this book is bounded by significant leaders: On the one end, introducing the book is a preface by Dr. Robert Rubinstein and on the other, a conclusion by Lieutenant General John E. Wissler.

**Dr. Robert Rubinstein** is the Distinguished Professor of Anthropology and Professor of International Relations at the Maxwell School of Syracuse University. Rubinstein is an anthropologist with expertise in political and medical anthropology and in social science history and research methods with a Ph.D. in Anthropology form the State University of New York at Binghampton. From 1994 to 2005 Rubinstein directed the Program on the Analysis and Resolution of Conflicts at the Maxwell School. Rubinstein has conducted overseas research in urban and rural Egypt, Belize, Mexico and in the United States. In political anthropology, Rubinstein's work focuses on cross-cultural aspects of conflict and dispute resolution, including negotiation, mediation and consensus building. Rubinstein has collaborated on policy applications of his work with the International Peace Academy, the United Nations Department of Peacekeeping Operations, and the United States Army Peacekeeping Institute. Rubinstein is the author of over 100 articles in journals and books and author or editor of nine books and research monographs as well as the recipient of numerous prestigious awards.

**Lieutenant General John Wissler** was raised in a Marine Family, settling in Brooklyn Park, Minnesota. He graduated from the United States Naval Academy and was commissioned a Second Lieutenant on June 7, 1978. He currently serves as Distinguished Chair of Leadership at the Stockdale Center for Ethical Leadership at the United States Naval Academy in Annapolis.

His company and field grade command assignments include landing support (shore party) and combat engineer platoons; three Combat Engineer companies; 2nd Combat Engineer Battalion; 2nd Transportation Support Battalion, and Task Force Pegasus supporting I MEF during OIF I. General Officer command assignments included 2nd FSSG (Fwd) and 2nd Marine Logistics Group; 2nd MEB; III Marine Expeditionary Force and Commander, Marine Corps Forces, Japan; and Commander, U.S. Marine Corps Forces Command and Commanding General, FMF Atlantic. While serving as CG, III MEF, Lieutenant General Wissler was twice activated as the Commander, Joint Task Force 505, conducting Humanitarian Assistance and Disaster Relief Operations in the Philippines in 2013 after super typhoon and during 2015 for earthquake relief in Nepal. Lieutenant general Wissler also served as Deputy CG, MNF-W during OIF 09 and Deputy CG, II MEF.

Staff assignments include Facilities Maintenance Officer MCRD, San Diego; Ops Officer 1st CEB and MWSG-17; CMC Amphibious Plans Study Group for Operation Desert Storm; Marine Corps Aide to the President; Division Engineer, 2nd Marine Division, Director, Strategic Initiatives Group; G-3, 2nd FSSG; Senior Military Assistant to the Deputy Secretary of Defense; and Deputy Commandant for Programs and Resources.

John graduated from the Amphibious Warfare School; the Air Force Institute of Technology (MS Industrial Engineering); Marine Corps Command and Staff College; Armed Forces Staff College; and served as a Commandant of the Marine Corps and Federal Executive Fellow at The Brookings Institution.

Lieutenant General Wissler is an Honorary Chief Petty Officer in the United States Navy and an Honorary Marine in the Republic of Korea Marine Corps, and has received the Order of the Rising Sun Gold and Silver Star from the Emperor of Japan; and the Order of National Security Merit, Gukseon Medal conferred by the President of the Republic of Korea.

Upon retirement from the Marine Corps, John has served as a consultant in the leadership development, team building, strategic planning and logistics fields, working with Industry, the military, professional sports teams and several colleges.

We, the authors are thankful to these exemplary leaders for their contributions.

Defining Culture for Leadership

# One

CLEMENTINE K. FUJIMURA

## INTRODUCTION: CULTURE AND BEHAVIOR

In the late 1980s I was among a wave of U.S. college students who had the opportunity to travel to the Soviet Union to study the Russian language. We freely roamed the streets of Moscow and Leningrad (today St. Petersburg) and befriended people who had been nearly impossible to meet prior to Mikhail Gorbachev's ascendance as General Secretary of the Communist Party (1985–1991). During our residence in university dormitories, some of us American students would rise early in the morning and go for a run before classes. Similar to our runs in the United States, we would encounter the waking up of a slumbering city. We could observe daily pre-work activities, such as markets opening and early morning street cleaning in front of public buildings. In Russia, this street cleaning was often performed by women—usually middle-aged or older—who wielded brooms made of branches. Excited to experience the novelties of Russia and hoping to demonstrate "American friendliness," we would smile at the women working, possibly offer a "*dobroe utro*" ("Good morning!") and run on. However, the response of the sweepers could be disconcerting; on more than one occasion, the women angrily shouted back—and even swiped at our legs.

What was going on? Were the women upset by our relatively skimpy running attire? Among Russians in those days, unlike today, it was uncommon for young woman to wear shorts or dare to be seen in a sweatsuit. Were they angry that we might be stepping into dirt they had swept into a pile? That didn't seem likely, since we took great pains to avoid the piles and the dust coming from sweeping brooms.

Obviously, given the frequency of the women's scowls, the situation had to be investigated further, as we did not want to offend the citizens of our host country. Ultimately, we discovered that the

DOI: 10.4324/9781003213352-2

women did not understand our smiles. Many of them assumed we were laughing at them. After all, why would anyone smile at a complete stranger? What was there to smile at? Life was tough in this place, we did not know one another, and we were demonstrating odd behavior by running in odd places, such as city streets, at an odd time, early in the morning before work. The cultural complexity involved in the moment of communication is perhaps more than this chapter can take on; however, what needs to be clear is that the response of the women was one that was steeped in culture—a culture that has behavioral expectations involving when and where to exercise, a culture that values close relations over superficial encounters, and one that over time has come to be suspicious of outsiders or behaviors that fall outside the norm. Running early in the morning, smiling, and offering a word (that may not have been comprehensible given our American accents) was simply not welcome, and indeed, perhaps shunned. As students coming to Russia, it would have been wise for us to learn in advance about local expectations in terms of public vs. private behaviors, and to identify which of our habits might be misconstrued or even found unacceptable.

This story demonstrates how cross-cultural communication (3C) can fail if the primary concept, culture, is not fully comprehended. By comprehended, I mean learned (apprehended), experienced (realized), and mentally and emotionally digested. While our experience was curious and potentially funny in hindsight, such miscommunication can impede more than one's morning run. Lacking an understanding of culture can interfere with the ability to build friendships, hinder business and diplomacy and destroy one's ability to lead, both at home and abroad. Culture is the fundamental concept necessary for building human relations.

Consider another example, this one involving an American businessman, "Mr. Anderson," who is working in Japan. He is offered a business card by a "Mr. Nakada." Happily, Mr. Anderson might take the card with one hand and even offer one in return, quickly and without much attention slipping Mr. Nakada's card into his back pocket. Mr. Nakada may only subtly reveal his consternation but continue the session by thanking Mr. Anderson, bowing, holding Mr. Anderson's card with two hands so that he may take a serious look at what it says, and, after sitting down, carefully placing it in front of him on the table. The resulting meeting may not go so well, unless Mr. Nakada is familiar with North American norms and realizes that to Mr. Anderson, the business card is just a piece of paper with information and that Mr. Anderson does not know that in Japan, the business card symbolizes one's identity. To carelessly take it without acknowledging the bearer's identity by reading it, and to put it in his back pocket to be sat upon, is truly offensive to the Japanese.

Once again, we see that similar behaviors might not mean the same thing to all. We see how the exchange of a card may reflect how a person demonstrates respect for another person and is not simply a paper transfer. We see that how we interact, our behaviors, are learned systems of meaning that reflect values that we communicate through symbolic systems such as language or rituals, for example.

Cultural behaviors should not be confused with actions based on an individual's psychology, which also influence the way we act in certain situations. We are not talking about how we interact based on our moods, emotions, cognition, or inherited personality traits, but rather on behavior that is learned and socialized. Of course, both culture and psychology intersect, a topic I might just leave for another day. Instead, I will focus on behavior that we learn throughout our lives, from when we are born to when we leave this planet—because we are social beings, because we communicate, because we interact. And so, we come to a definition of culture as:

> an orchestration of learned systems of meaning that are communicated, negotiated, and adapted via language and other symbolic systems. These systems of meaning contain representational, directive, and affective functions, create unique understandings of reality, and structure interpersonal relations and activities.
> (Significantly adapted from d'Andrade, 1984: 116)

This definition is complex but revealing. It points to the fact that people learn how to make sense of reality in different ways, depending on their culture, and that they perpetuate these ways but also adapt to changes occurring as a result of interpersonal exchanges and communications. Expectations in relationships depend on the degree to which people understand each other's cultures. For, as soon as Mr.

Anderson made his faux pas, his relationship with Mr. Nakada was problematized, leading to a variety of potential outcomes affecting future business relations, and views the two men hold of each other and of each other's societies—for good or for bad.

Culture, as we have come to understand it in English,[1] offers us a rubric for explaining reality, experiencing the world and guiding our behaviors. The shared systems of meaning of a society or community can be understood as conscious and subconscious paradigms that help us perceive ourselves, the world around us, and others. Let's take an example throughout which I will ask you to check in with your feelings and explore your judgments.

- This is the story of a 30-something businessman, who earns approximately $90,000 a year. How would you score this man? In many cultures, including our own, this man's life looks promising if not excellent.
- Now you find out that he is unmarried and enjoys meeting women on a dating app, but that he has not been in a long-term relationship since college. Now what do you think about him? Some of us would think that's normal since it is difficult to meet people these days. Others might feel that he is slow to settle down, which might lead to an evaluation of his character.
- Then you find out that he is living at home with his parents. Now how do you feel? How does this information go against what makes sense to you, that is, challenge your system of meaning or what you think is right, wrong, good or bad? In the United States, this man's standing just dropped a great deal. Would you even hire him? Of course, there may be reasons why he lives at home with his parents.

While our culture values individualism and independence, which can be achieved to varying degrees depending on one's age, gender, education, and income, other cultures value collectivism, which would expect children, no matter what their age, to live with their parents and take care of them (this exercise was adapted from Sorrells, 2015: 5–6).

Geert Hofstede, a Dutch social psychologist and anthropologist, developed a cultural dimensions theory in which he describes how a nation's value tendencies influence all levels of a society (state or nation). One of these dimensions is the Individualism Index, which he defines as pertaining

> to societies in which the ties between individuals are loose; everyone is expected to look after himself or herself and his or her immediate family. Collectivism as its opposite pertains to societies in which throughout, people from birth onward are integrated into strong, cohesive in-groups, which throughout people's lifetimes continue to protect them in exchange for unquestioning loyalty.
>
> (Öncer, 2013: 105)

Cultures that value individualism are concerned with freedom of the individual to develop and thrive independently, whereas collectivistic cultures emphasize interdependence.

In contrast to our emphasis on independence in the United States, Russian culture abides by a system of shared meanings that values kinship relations and taking care of each other in a family, often leading to co-habitation. Grandparents, and in particular grandmothers, are frequently the caretakers of grandchildren while parents work outside the home. Co-habitation is completely normal. Expectations within families are intertwined with beliefs about gender roles, education and the like. While grandfathers may assist in taking care of grandchildren, grandmothers are the nurturers.

When it comes to our 30-something's dating situation, again, the shared systems of meaning that evaluate his philandering vary from culture to culture. In the United States, we might excuse it given his preoccupation with establishing his independence financially, or because it's his life, he can do what he wants, right? In a more collectivist society, expectations of settling down might be more significant.

Shared meanings, a complex of intertwined values such as expectations of what makes a good offspring (success, independence, and the like) give us rules as well as biases, with boundaries and a sense of security in the familiar and communal connectedness. In the end, culture shapes our worldview—that is, how we perceive and construe cognitively and emotionally our experiences and make sense of our world around us (see Value rubrics).

## CULTURE AS RUBRIC

In trying to detect and understand when culture is impacting events, we can use the iceberg metaphor for initial, albeit rather superficial, guidance: At the tip of the iceberg we see the results of culture, such as artifacts, foods, dress and art, to list a few. At the middle level, we may be receptive to traditions, customs and less obvious symbolic communication. Supporting all of this is the vast bottom of the iceberg, which contains the origins of, and motivations for, the upper levels: beliefs, values, ideology and the like (see Figure 1.1).

Behaviors are shaped by the bottom of the iceberg: the core values, assumptions about common sense, the concept of self and others, and

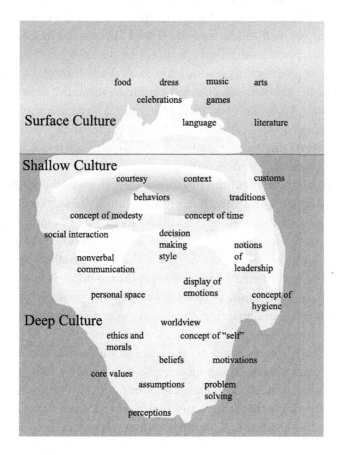

**Figure 1.1** Iceberg

worldview. While some people may not be open to questioning their behavior due to the deep-rootedness of their cultural motivations, the practice of self-questioning is valuable for leaders. Being attuned to one's own and others' behavioral similarities and differences as cultural outcomes can influence a leader's capacity to influence performance, work satisfaction and growth, all of which has the potential to positively affect an organization's culture.

## A BRIEF HISTORY OF THE CULTURE CONCEPT

The interpretation of the culture concept has been debated historically and to this day there is no one definition of "culture." Rather it is a complex concept that continues to be explained, depending on the context in which it is being used. Indeed, the process of defining culture is, in and of itself, a cultural process (Stocking, 1966: 867). The concept as we tend to use it in the United States is one that evolved out of anthropological inquiry and scholarship and is an outcome of American anthropology, with Franz Boas as the informal founder. Unlike earlier scholars who defined culture in absolutist, even evolutionist ways, Boas tends toward a relativistic interpretation, with all people being equally "cultured" (see Stocking, 1966: 868). Definitions aside, however, the culture concept has evolved in the social sciences as being essential to understanding human behavior.

While a notion of culture first began to develop in the 19th century in Germany, and subsequently the United States, the concept as it is debated today arose from Boas' ideas about "cultural relativism," introduced around 1910—i.e., that cultures cannot be ranked objectively as higher or lower than one another, and that one culture is not better or more correct than another. While earlier, evolutionary approaches to culture held that all societies progress through a series of hierarchic steps, Boas got us to talk instead about smaller, unique groups of people (see Stocking, 1966: 871). This idea that each society has developed due to a unique historical past and that each society can develop to the same level by following its unique paths, which may (and today in our globally connected time most likely will) include interactions with other societies, was coined "historical particularism," another term developed by Boas and his students.

Scholars have continued to define, refine and redefine culture. In 2006, a survey found 313 scholarly definitions of culture, with each definition depending on its frame of reference:

1. *Structure/pattern*—culture as a system or framework of elements (e.g., ideas, behavior, symbols or any combination of these or other elements)
2. *Function*—culture as a means for achieving some end
3. *Process*—culture as an ongoing process of social construction
4. *Product*—culture as a collection of artifacts (with or without deliberate symbolic intent)
5. *Refinement*—culture as individual or group cultivation to higher intellect or morality
6. *Group membership*—culture as signifying a place or group of people, including a focus on belonging to a place or group
7. *Power or ideology*—culture as an expression of group-based domination and power.

(Faulkner, Baldwin, Lindsley, & Hecht, 2006: 29–30 in Weil 2017)

In his elaboration of the culture concept, Nolan Weil (2017) offers a narrative to comment on the diversity of definitions:

Six blind men confronting an elephant for the first time came away from the experience with six different descriptions, owing to their different angles of approach. One blind man, reaching up to touch the animal's broad side, concluded that the elephant was like a wall. Another man, running into a leg, decided that an elephant was like a tree. A third man seizing the elephant's trunk, proclaimed the elephant to be a snake, while the fourth man grasping the tail, declared the elephant to be more like a rope. Meanwhile, a fifth man grasping the ear was sure the elephant was like a fan, while the sixth man encountering a tusk was equally sure the elephant was a spear. Only by bringing all of the separate parts of the elephant together could anyone hope to acquire a complete and coherent impression of an elephant. Perhaps culture is a bit like this. Our concept of it is enriched when we are able to see it from many different angles.

(Weil, 2017)

Each definition offers something for us to ponder. Clifford Geertz's definition of culture motivated anthropologists to see culture as a web of meanings. He saw culture as "a system of inherited conceptions expressed in symbolic forms by means of which men communicate, perpetuate, and develop their knowledge about and attitudes toward life" (Geertz, 1973). In other words, culture is comprised of meanings people create to make sense of their lives and to guide their actions. This definition allows for a more fluid and less static approach to understanding culture. Geertz's definition sees behavior as only the drama of a much deeper meaning-making process. Behavior is only one tip of an iceberg.

A leader might be particularly drawn to the definition of culture as an expression of group-based domination and power. American anthropologist Eric Wolf (1923–1999) was of particular significance to initiating scholarly understanding of the role that power plays in influencing our definitions of culture and understanding cultural change and social oppression. He contended that previous definitions of culture assumed a bounded entity rather than acknowledging culture change as due to other, more dominant societies. Even diffusionists (as in Boas' definition), he argued, described cultures as integrated entities and as nouns. Wolf underscored the fact that a culture's core can be the direct outcome of goals of dominant groups that manipulate symbols and structures to perpetuate domination (see Schoenmakers, 2012: 74–76). In this sense, one might see culture as a web of meanings, as Geertz would have it, and moreover, as a contested process of meaning-making. It is a contest in which players define, negotiate, and justify terms, concepts and relationships. As a result, culture is a power process (Ibid.: 95–96).

Not everyone would agree that culture is all about power relations. Indeed, common use of the term goes back to the definition I offered above: as a learned system of meaning that is communicated, negotiated and adapted via language and other symbolic systems and which contains representational, directive and affective functions that create unique understandings of reality and that structure interpersonal relations and activities. However, for leaders, understanding the power one has in a leadership position in affecting culture change is imperative to being cross-culturally competent.

## CULTURE AND COMMUNICATION

Culture would be insignificant if we did not have a means by which to communicate. Understanding the complexity of communication is equally important to understanding the complexity of culture. Communication happens on many levels, from nonverbal communications to verbal language. Verbal language is one of the main ways by which we send and receive messages. However, it is not universal: Our language is a unique product of our culture and in turn, culture is a product of our language: Language influences, maintains and alters our systems of meaning.

Language influences what and how we see and think. It is a system of arbitrary symbols that human beings use to encode their experience of the world and to communicate with one another. Depending on the words we use and can imagine as standing for specific ideas, we are able to perceive those ideas. For example, if I say seaweed, what comes to mind? How many variations of seaweed can you come up with? If you lived by the ocean you might picture a couple or more. Do you have words for them? In Japan, there are numerous words for seaweed, each conjuring up a different image: *nori, konbu, hijiki, wakame* and *mozuku*, for example. These are all as distinct as saying lettuce, cabbage and spinach. Moreover, people utilizing seaweed for healing associate different healing potential to each type of seaweed. Their perception of seaweed—its multifarious nature and distinct powers—allows them to perceive seaweed differently than we might.[2]

But beyond what we can learn in a textbook, it is the spoken language, the utterance of the textbook version of language along with non-verbal communication, which is equally and perhaps more important to understanding culture. How people think about themselves and the world around them is communicated mostly in speech and nonverbal communication, not in the standardized form of a language.[3] It is the iteration of language in verbal and body language, including dialect, that gives us insight into aptitudes, underlying sentiments, humor, pride and motivations. According to a famous study in 1967, Albert Mehrabian found that, depending on the context, the history between people, and their role in communicating (e.g., boss vs. employee), and specifically when talking about emotions, 55% of communication was concluded to be nonverbal (body movements such as raising eyebrows, movement of the mouth and fidgeting), 38% was tone of voice, and just 7% was the actual words spoken (Mehrabian, 2009). Since then his study has often been misinterpreted, with many claiming body language to be the most important conveyer of messages in all communications—regardless of context, history of relationships, and individual players' roles. At the very least, studies have alerted us to the significance of nonverbal communication in everyday interactions.

What is indisputable is that to truly understand a culture, knowing the language in its fullest expression, from text to verbal to nonverbal iterations, is important. The ability to understand why, what and how people communicate brings us closest to gaining an insider's perspective (the emic perspective) as opposed to a tourist's glance (the etic perspective).

### TAKEAWAYS FOR THE LEADER IN DEFINING CULTURE

In any organization, one encounters individuals with diverse reasons and motivations for engaging based on their experiences and values. Acknowledging these differences as valuable to the organization entails the following:

- Knowing that cultural backgrounds run deep. While adaptability of all individuals to the organizational culture can be aspirational, change is difficult.
- Understanding that you, too, function based on your own culture or cultures: You have culture too, and it is complicated. Understanding where you are coming from is just as important as learning about and understanding others.
- Recognizing when a behavior or event is cultural. This requires a leader to take time to learn about the motivations and to adapt in (often uncomfortable) interactions.
- Comprehending (apprehend, realize and digest) a culture. This is best accomplished through immersion and experience in that culture.
- Taking time to understand a language because it will bring you more deeply into the cultural perspectives of individuals and allow for more seamless communication and leadership.

- Realizing that cultural diversity can enhance an organization's effectiveness and ultimate success by offering a greater range of talent, if the leadership is cross-culturally competent.
- Appreciating that power influences interactions, from a cultural perspective as well as from individual perspectives.

## CULTURAL SELF-ASSESSMENT

1. When was the last time I recognized a behavior or interaction as cultural or as different from how I would have acted? How was it due to culture?
2. When did I immerse myself in a foreign space or society? What was immersive about the experience? How could it have been more immersive?
3. What can I do to experiment with new situations and appreciate power interactions, cultural interactions and differences in communication? (Example: I could venture to a new neighborhood, either in person or online, and interact with individuals with a goal in mind: to purchase something, to help someone, to learn something).
4. Reflect on your experiment.

## NOTES

1 It must be noted that the term "culture" is not a universal concept. For example, even though the German word "Kultur" and the Polish word "kultura" resemble the English "culture," there are important differences in meaning, and in more distant languages like Mandarin Chinese (wen hua), we might expect the differences to be even greater (Goddard, 2005 in Weil, 2017).
2 Edward Sapir and Lee Whorf in 1929 came up with the Sapir–Whorf hypothesis that argued that the structure of language determines a native speaker's perception and ordering of experiences. Whorf explains: "The categories and types that weisolate from the world ofphenomena wedo not find there because they stare every observer in the face. On the contrary, the world is presented in a kaleidoscopic flux of impressions which have to be organized in our minds. This means, largely, by the linguistic system in our minds (Whorf, 1956 (1940): 212ffl).
3 This distinction between "langue" and "parole" was introduced by Ferdinand de Saussure (1857–1913), in which langue is the system of language that makes parole possible. Parole is the actual shape langue takes when uttered. It is the use of the system.

## REFERENCES

d'Andrade, R. G. (1984). Cultural meaning systems. In Culture theory: Essays on mind, self, and emotion. Cambridge: Cambridge University Press.

Faulkner, S. L., Baldwin, J. R., Lindsley, S. L., & Hecht, M. L. (2006). Layers of meaning: An analysis of definitions of culture. In Redefining culture: Perspectives across the disciplines. Mahwah, NJ: Lawrence Erlbaum.

Geertz, C. (1973). The interpretation of cultures: Selected essays. New York: Basic Books.

Goddard, C. (2005). The lexical semantics of "culture." Language Sciences, 27, 51–73. https://doi.org/10.1016/j.langsci.2004.05.001

Mehrabian, A. (2009). Silent messages: A wealth of information about nonverbal communication (body language). Personality & Emotion Tests & Software: Psychological Books & Articles of Popular Interest. Los Angeles: self-published.

Öncer, A. Z. (2013). The relationship between individualism–collectivism and organizations' espoused values. The Business & Management Review, 3(3), March, 105–114.

Schoenmakers, H. (2012). The power of culture: A short history of anthropological theory about culture and power. Retrieved from www.rug.nl/research/globalisation-studies-groningen/publications/researchreports/reports/powerofculture.pdf

Sorrells, K. (2015). Intercultural communication: Globalization and social justice. Thousand Oaks, CA: Sage.

Stocking, G. (1966). Franz Boas and the culture concept in historical perspective. American Anthropologist, New Series, 68(4), August, 867–882.

Value rubrics, The Association of American Colleges and Universities (AAC&U) Critical Thinking VALUE Rubric. Retrieved from www.aacu.org/value-rubrics, viewed March 8, 2020.

Whorf, B. L. (1956[1940]). Science and linguistics. In John B. Carroll (Ed.), Language, thought and reality: Selected writings of Benjamin Lee Whorf. Cambridge, MA: MIT.

Weil, N. (2017). Speaking of culture. Salt Lake City, UT: Utah State University. Retrieved from https://press.rebus.community/originsofthehumanfamily/

# Two

JOSEPH J. THOMAS

## THE GLOBE STUDY: THE CULTURE CONNECTION TO
## LEADER EFFECTIVENESS

In over 25 years of teaching, thinking and writing about leadership and nearly 40 years of being a practicing leader, I've come to a sobering realization: *This stuff is hard!* It's difficult to generalize about leadership— as an activity, it's tailored to an organization's context, mission and place. Leadership in private sector organizations differs from that in the public sector, and even in the public sector it varies according to the mission. Leadership exercised at the State Department differs from that exercised at the Justice Department, which is different from the Department of Defense.

Leadership is often valued differently than management, particularly because methods to develop competence in each vary significantly. While there are many ways to define both, my personal background leads me to define leader development as honing the sum of those qualities of intellect, human understanding and moral character in order to enable a person to inspire and influence a group of people to accomplish missions and solve problems. Leadership focuses on interpersonal interactions with the purpose of increasing organizational effectiveness. This added emphasis on organizational effectiveness is by way of individual effectiveness.

Management, on the other hand, is a process that results in getting other people to execute proscribed formal duties for organizational goal attainment. As a process, it is focused primarily on efficiency. Both leadership and management are critical organizational functions, and some mistakenly believe that management is somehow inferior to leadership. For our purposes, we'll consider management a narrower, formulaic component of leadership.

If *culture* is comprised of meanings people create to make sense of their lives and to guide their actions, and *leadership* is the process

DOI: 10.4324/9781003213352-3

by which one directs, influences and inspires the efforts of others toward a common purpose, then how are the two concepts related? That question is exhaustively answered in the "Global Leadership and Organizational Behavior Effectiveness" (GLOBE) Research Program (House et al., 2004). Conceived initially at the Wharton School of Business at the University of Pennsylvania in 1991 by Robert J. House, it built upon the work of Geert Hofstede and others in classifying similarities and differences in beliefs, values and practices across cultures.

The first phase of the massive study focused on the development of research instruments designed to explore the relationship between organizational and societal culture—for our purposes this is the very nexus of culture and leadership. The second phase was devoted to the assessment of nine core attributes of organizational and societal culture. Those core attributes or cultural dimensions are:

**Table 2.1** Core attributes or cultural dimensions

| | |
|---|---|
| **Power Distance** | The degree to which members of a collective expect power to be distributed equally. |
| **Uncertainty Avoidance** | The extent to which a society, organization or group relies on social norms, rules and procedures to alleviate unpredictability of future events. |
| **Humane Orientation** | The degree to which a collective encourages and rewards individuals for being fair, altruistic, generous, caring and kind to others. |
| **Collectivism I (Institutional)** | The degree to which organizational and societal institutional practices encourage and reward collective distribution of resources and collective action. |
| **Collectivism II (In-Group)** | The degree to which individuals express pride, loyalty and cohesiveness in their organizations or families. |
| **Assertiveness** | The degree to which individuals are assertive, confrontational and aggressive in their relationships with others. |
| **Gender Egalitarianism** | The degree to which a collective minimizes gender inequality. |
| **Future Orientation** | The extent to which individuals engage in future-oriented behaviors such as delaying gratification, planning and investing in the future. |
| **Performance Orientation** | The degree to which a collective encourages and rewards group members for performance improvement and excellence. |

Adapted from Center for Creative Leadership "Leader Effectiveness and Culture: The Globe Study," 2012.

## THE 21 LEADERSHIP SCALES AND SIX STYLES

One of the most common questions that preface any leader development conversation is, *"Are leaders born or are they made?"* Audiences in the 21st century, particularly in the United States, are likely to answer "made." Generally, there is a strong cultural belief across the West that holds anyone can be developed into a better, if not great, leader. This belief, however, is a very recent phenomenon, even in the West. For centuries, historians and philosophers suggested that the best way to impart leadership lessons was through the careful study of those who "got it right." In 1840, a Scottish historian named Thomas Carlyle introduced "The Great Man Theory" through a book and series of lectures entitled, *On Heroes, Hero-Worship, and the Heroic in History.* Carlyle profiled great men throughout history and pointed out certain attributes that, when studied carefully and methodically, could be instructive to aspiring leaders. This approach is found in Plutarch's *Lives,* a series of biographies of great leaders from the ancient world. Plato's Philosopher–King, Machiavelli's Prince, Hobbes' Sovereign and Nietzsche's Ubermensch are all embodiments of perfect leaders observed.

The principal drawback to this thesis is that there's an implied suggestion that some are simply born to lead. This theory of hereditary dominance has been rightly discarded by modern theorists in most cultures, although echoes of it are still found in the work of contemporary theorists such as Harvard University's Howard Gardner, countless biographical historians and many of the world's militaries. The study of the biographies of Great Captains and their campaigns still dominates the curricula of most major military schools throughout the world today. However, today this so-called "Great Man Theory" and the Trait Theory of Leadership it spawned have been augmented by other paradigms.

In the early 20th century, behaviorists such as Max Weber, Ralph Stogdill and Kurt Lewin rejected traits as the basis for explaining leader development and began to define replicable behaviors. This meant that leadership could be studied, practiced and mastered. Ohio State conducted an extensive research project shortly after World War II on the leadership of aircrews during the war. The study seemed to confirm the behaviorist approach, and the high consideration/high structure styles at the heart of the behaviorists' work eventually prevailed.

Similar studies were replicated in other parts of the world and this approach became, in essence, an accepted global view in spite of its poor fit with many cultures.

In the 21st century, the dominant approach derived from the work of the behaviorists is competency based. Competence is typically defined as the knowledge, skills, abilities and aptitudes necessary to complete a given task. Competency-based models of leader development and assessment have become particularly popular in the West because they offer observable, measurable methods to encourage leader improvement. The GLOBE Study is an extension of this belief and tests its principles in a cross-cultural environment. Where GLOBE is utterly unique is in its broad capture of cultural differences affecting leadership practice.

The theoretical framework of the GLOBE Study[1] is rooted in the belief that the personal qualities of the leader must fit the expectations of followers. Those expectations constrain, moderate and guide the exercise of leadership. Followers grant status and privilege to leaders who meet their expectations. GLOBE measures follower expectations in 21 leadership "scales," or behavioral qualities, that can be ranked according to cultural beliefs and tendencies. The 21 leadership scales, ranked from "most universally desired" across all world cultures to "least universally desired," are:

Integrity: Honest, sincere, just, trustworthy
Inspirational: Enthusiastic, positive, morale booster, motive arouser
Visionary: Foresight, prepared, anticipatory, plans ahead
Performance-oriented: Improvement-oriented, excellence-oriented
Team-integrator: Communicative, team-builder, integrator
Decisive: Willful, decisive, logical, intuitive
Administratively competent: Orderly, organized, good administrator
Diplomatic: Win/win problem solver, effective bargainer
Collaborative: Team orientation
Self-sacrificial: risk taker, self-sacrificial, convincing
Modesty: Self-effacing, patient
Humane orientation: Generous, compassionate
Status conscious: Aware of one's own or class standing
Conflict inducer: Normative, secretive, intra-group competitor
Procedural: Ritualistic, formal, habitual

*Autonomous*: Individualistic, independent, unique

*Face saver*: Indirect, avoids negatives, evasive

*Non-participative*: Non-delegator, micro-manager, non-egalitarian

*Autocratic*: Dictatorial, bossy, elitist

*Self-centered*: Non-participative, loner, asocial

*Malevolent*: Hostile, dishonest, vindictive, irritable.

These 21 scales were categorized into six styles within the GLOBE Study. Cultural preference for each style varies greatly, often in surprising ways. Most importantly, GLOBE introduced empirical evidence that follower expectations were driven in very large part by cultural dynamics. This came as a surprise to some since Western (primarily U.S.) researchers had done the vast majority of the research concerning leader effectiveness. This research, quite naturally, had previously been done using an almost exclusively Western-focused lens.

The following styles are listed in order of "least cultural variation/most universal" to "most cultural variation/least universal":

1. **The charismatic/value-based style** stresses high standards, decisiveness, and innovation; seeks to inspire people around a vision; creates a passion among them to perform; and does so by firmly holding on to core values. This includes the facets of visionary, inspirational, self-sacrificial, integrity, decisive and performance-oriented.

2. **The team-oriented style** instills pride, loyalty and collaboration among organizational members; and highly values team cohesiveness and a common purpose or goals. This style includes the facets of collaborative team orientation, team integrator, diplomatic, (reverse scored) malevolent and administratively competent.

3. **The participative style** encourages input from others in decision-making and implementation and emphasizes delegation and equality. This style includes the facets of (reverse scored) autocratic and (reverse scored) non-participative.

4. **The humane style** stresses compassion and generosity; and it is patient, supportive and concerned with the well-being of others. This style includes the facets of modesty and humane-oriented.

5. **The self-protective** style emphasizes procedural, status-conscious, and "face-saving" behaviors and focuses on the safety and security

of the individual and the group. This style includes the facets of self-centered, status-conscious, conflict inducer, face saver and procedural.

6. **The autonomous style** includes only one aspect of autonomy. It is characterized by an independent, individualistic and self-centric approach to leadership.

### VARIED CULTURAL EXPECTATIONS OF LEADERSHIP: CULTURE CLUSTERS

The practices (the way things are done) and values (the way things should be done) of 62 societies were surveyed in the GLOBE Study. Researchers then asked, "How is culture related to societal, organizational, and leadership effectiveness?" Some 27 hypotheses linking

## Culture Clusters in the GLOBE Study

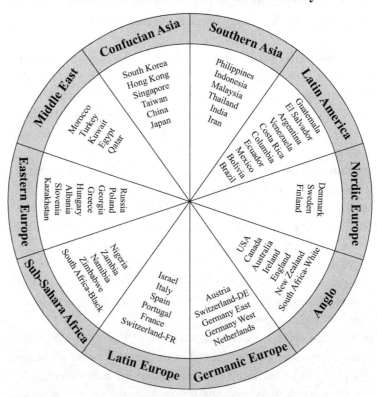

**Figure 2.1** Culture clusters in the GLOBE Study

culture to leadership outcomes were tested, with 17,300 managers in 951 organizations participating. Culture clusters were derived from the findings of the research. The figure below depicts the grouping of similar societies and labels by geographic/cultural influence. The further each wedge is from another indicates cultural difference. For example, Anglo culture differs in significant ways from Middle Eastern culture, and Southern Asia culture differs significantly from Latin Europe culture, while Anglo culture differs less from Germanic Europe cultures, and Southern Asia culture differs less from Confucian Asia cultures.

## OTHER DIMENSIONS OF CULTURE

The GLOBE Study determined that views of what constitutes effective leadership are contextual. Cultural dimensions determine how people view the actions of leaders. Cultures that score high in assertiveness, for example, expect leaders to be direct even to the point of aggressiveness. Alternatively, cultures that score low in assertiveness expect leaders to collaborate and encourage cooperative conversations. Understanding dimensions of cultural value not only helps us to compare cultures, but that understanding can guide our behaviors and beliefs to better fit a culture with which we interact. Observing patterns of behavior in leaders according to these cultural dimensions can be key to organizational success. While there are many dimensions of cultural value, I will list those I believe are essential to cross-cultural competence. Each dimension represents a continuum and will, therefore, be presented as a scale between two extremes.

### Tight vs. Loose Social Norms (Gelfand, 2011)

A norm is a standard or pattern, especially of social behavior, that is typical or expected of a group. Those who have traveled internationally quickly realize there are few universal social norms. The strength to which a culture adheres to social norms also varies widely. Some cultures have little tolerance for those who deviate from standard social behavior. Many researchers believe this cultural dimension is changing more quickly than any other because of globalization and the perceived emergence of a homogenous global cultural culture. While there is some evidence for this, the vast majority of the world still operates on very local patterns of social behavior.

"Tight" cultures are generally, but not exclusively, found in isolated places. Adherence to norms, rules, and standards in tight cultures is often enforced in direct and indirect ways. For example, in one of the tightest cultures in the world, that of Saudi Arabia, social norms are policed by the government-sanctioned Committee for the Promotion of Virtue and Prevention of Vice. Nearly 4,000 public morality police, referred to as *mutaween*, are aided by tens of thousands of volunteers in ensuring public decency is upheld across the kingdom. Punishment for even unintentional deviations from expected social etiquette can be quite severe. Less severe examples of tight cultures are found in places like Japan and France, where improper dining etiquette may result in nothing more than social judgment.

On the other end of the scale, "loose" cultures are generally, but not exclusively, found in places shaped by cross-cultural inter-action. For example, the Netherlands, one of the loosest cultures in the world, served as a crossroad of cultures dating back to Iron Age Europe. Celts, Gauls, Vikings, Romans and others exercised influence over the Low Countries through the Early Middle Ages. The Spanish and Germans would later occupy the Netherlands and throughout its history it served as a center of trade between the Old and New World. The United States and Canada tend toward loose social norms but for entirely different reasons. Both have long histories of immigration and assimilation of various cultures.

Of all the dimensions, cross-cultural education can play a key role in leadership or even social success. It is important for travelers from loose cultures to be aware of, and respectful toward, cultural beliefs of tight cultures. That's not to say one must personally embrace the morality or spiritual beliefs often found in tight cultures—but awareness and respect are key.

### Low vs. High Power Distance (Hofstede, 1991)

One of Hofstede's original constructs for considering cultural differences, power distance, has obvious implications for leaders. Power distance beliefs define how people think about the distribution of wealth, submit to authority and accord privileges of status to others. High power distance cultures have higher levels of inequality and are more willing to accept that differences among people are

**Table 2.2** Key differences of beliefs within this cultural dimension

| Low Power Distance | High Power Distance |
| --- | --- |
| Inequalities among people are minimized. | Inequalities among people are expected and desired. |
| All members of society treat each other as equals. | Respect is basic and lifelong virtue. |
| Decentralization is popular. | Centralization is popular. |
| Subordinates expect to be consulted. | Subordinates expect to be told what to do. |
| The ideal boss is a resourceful democrat. | The ideal boss is a benevolent autocrat. |
| Manual work has the same status as office work. | White-collar jobs are valued more than blue-collar jobs. |
| Mostly wealthier countries with large middle class. | Mostly poorer countries with a small middle class. |
| All should have equal rights. | The powerful should have privileges. |
| There are small income differentials in society, further reduced by the tax system. | There are large income differentials in society, further increased by the tax system. |
| There are fewer supervisory personnel. | There are more supervisory personnel. |

naturally occurring phenomena. Low power distance cultures have lower levels of inequality and are less willing to accept unequal power distribution. These cultures tend to value individualism and representative governments. Table 2.2 illustrates the key differences of beliefs within this cultural dimension.

Low power distance countries like Sweden or Israel can be confusing places for travelers from high power distance countries. There seems to be no hierarchy or structure to help navigate relationships. Informality in inter-personal relationships is the guiding principle. In high power distance countries such as Morocco, South Korea or India, travelers from low power distance countries can feel stifled or constrained by protocol.

Interestingly, the very concept of leadership itself is more fully embraced in high power distance countries. Merely asking questions may be interpreted as subversion. Charismatic and even autocratic styles of leadership find acceptance in these cultures. In more egalitarian, low power distance cultures, people tend to value participative styles of leadership. If, as the futurist Thomas L. Friedman suggests in *The World is Flat*, modern means of communication will increasingly influence organizational structure and make business as well as societies "flatter," then the future for global culture will tend toward low power distance, enabling the empowerment of traditionally marginalized groups within every society. The arbitrary use of power by authoritarian governments or religious institutions will become more difficult. As long as power and status are prized human values, however, people and institutions will push in the other direction.

### Low vs. High Uncertainty Avoidance

One of the great causes of anxiety in people is uncertainty about the future. Individual dispositions tend to affect how people cope with ambiguity, but societies tend to encourage philosophical or spiritual dispositions to cope with that unknowable future. Uncertainty avoidance reflects a society's general tolerance for risk. Cultures with high uncertainty avoidance tend to resist change, are intolerant of non-traditional practices, enjoy structure, build rigid systems of rules, and are defined by formal interactions among people. Germany and Italy are high uncertainty avoidance countries, and many attribute this to the legacy of the culture of the Roman Empire—a culture defined by its structure, laws and unending quest to control the future. This is not to say people from these countries avoid risky behavior—both are known for fast cars and other artifacts of dangerous pursuit of entertainment.

Cultures low in uncertainty avoidance tend to be characterized by informality in interpersonal interactions and place higher value on innovation and originality. Above all, they prefer to let the future play out without a desire to control its outcomes. They are open to new ideas and rely on informal norms to guide behavior. Situations are dealt with as they arise. Examples of countries that score low on uncertainty avoidance are Jamaica, Ireland and Denmark.

If you are from a high uncertainty avoidance culture, it's helpful to keep in mind that you may seem dogmatic, judgmental and controlling to those from low uncertainty avoidance cultures. Asking open-ended questions is an excellent way to start conversations. Accept that punctuality is culturally driven and lack of it likely not meant as a personal affront. Conversely, those from low uncertainty avoidance cultures should be aware that deviating from the pre-agreed upon plan can be disorienting to people from high uncertainty avoidance cultures. Be prepared to give and receive detailed instructions, but also realize that too many questions can seem disrespectful.

### Individual vs. Collective Identity (Iyengar et al., 1999)

Collectivism prioritizes group interest over self-interest and is often seen as a political philosophy as much as a cultural dimension. It forms the center point of communism and, to a lesser degree, socialism. Individualism, on the other hand, prioritizes autonomy, self-determined merit and personal liberty. China is usually considered the country best representing collective cultural identity, while the United States is considered the best representative example of individualistic culture. Objective research in this dimension consistently bears this out. In a world characterized by a great and growing power competition between these two nations, there is little doubt these identities are one of the most important cultural dimensions for leaders in every sector to bear in mind.

Children raised in collectivist cultures are taught that the worth of their achievements will be measured primarily by their contribution to societal good. Kinship models drive choices. One's identity is typically defined by matters of birth, heritage and obligation to family. The Chinese concept of *mianzi* (面子) or "face" is also closely associated with this cultural dimension in that it refers to self-respect derived from social standing and recognition. This dimension influences nearly every aspect of life, in that it determines perceptions of success. The urge for belonging to something larger than yourself permeates collectivist cultures. The pace of life is generally slow in relation to individualistic cultures.

Children raised in individualistic cultures are taught to make the most of themselves. They will be defined by their choices more than other factors if they are to "make a mark in the world." As an educator from the United States, who travels internationally with students from the United States, I have found this dimension an incredibly powerful teaching tool about cultural assumptions. Most of my students have assumed all people measure their worth by their achievements and accomplishments. They rarely see connections to forbearers—or even fellow citizens—in the choices they make. My students have rarely seen the interdependence of the variables associated with their accomplishments. They see their individual talent and work ethic as determining all outcomes. Achievement is usually seen as an end in itself and being true to yourself as a guiding principle. The pace of life is generally much faster in relation to collectivist cultures.

### Cooperative vs. Competitive

Like the individual vs. collective identity cultural dimension, the cooperative vs. competitive dimension reflects how one prioritizes common good. A cooperative orientation is characterized by reciprocal relationships and collaborative behavior. Sensitivity to the feelings of others is factored in greatly in decision-making. Consensus is prized and the welfare of all concerned is emphasized. Coexistence and harmony are valued.

Competitive cultures encourage individuals to be their personal best because only the toughest win and the fittest survive. Collaboration is prized but only insofar as it can be crafted into a "win/win." Time is money. Communication should be honest, straightforward and efficient. Building high performing teams is optimal because they represent the best opportunities for everyone, but they are not an end in themselves. It is the result that matters most in the competitive worldview.

When engaged in inter-cultural interactions, particularly if negotiating, it is important to understand that cooperative vs. competitive is not necessarily binary. Egalitarian cultures such as Thailand, Finland and Norway prioritize compromise and are most willing to meet in the middle. "Win/win" cultures reflect elements of both cooperation and competitiveness. The United States, much of Western and Central Europe, India, Japan and Latin America tend to prefer this negotiating style. In Russia, Ukraine and most Eastern European countries, negotiations often take a very adversarial tone. Pressure tactics and aggressive language are typically part of every serious negotiation. China, South Korea, Pakistan and most of the Middle Eastern cultures usually prefer a combination of competitiveness and cooperation. Negotiators from these countries rarely concern themselves with the other side's outcomes. Rather, they'll develop a predetermined and prioritized list of acceptable terms and will only walk away from negotiations if they're unable to reach a threshold of acceptable terms (Katz, 2014).

### Being vs. Doing

One of the cultural dimensions most subject to internal scrutiny is the concept of "being" vs. "doing." "Being" cultures value relationships and quality of life. Lines between work and play can often become blurred, and priority is often given to time away from task accomplishment. In "being" cultures, one works to live, rather than lives to work. The role of work and the use of time are meant to serve a larger purpose. Many Middle Eastern, Nordic, Latin American and African cultures fit this pattern. Many of those same cultures are examining this dynamic so that that they can become more competitive with "doing" cultures in the global marketplace. "Being" cultures are often perceived as being laid back and less productive.

"Doing" cultures, on the other hand, value accomplishment, being productive and maximizing the use of time. The United States, Japan and Singapore are strong "doing" cultures. Many people in "doing" cultures live to work and often skip available vacation days in order get everything done. These beliefs and values are being questioned, particularly by the young, in "doing" cultures—witness the widespread use of "work/life balance" programming in corporate settings, for example. Sacrificing one's personal life for professional demands is far less common among the younger generation, even in the most strident "doing" cultures.

One of the greatest impacts of the "being" vs. "doing" dimension is the varying orientations toward time. In the United States and much of the developed world, our schedules are typically organized around specified time agreements. The clock determines when things should begin and end. As globalization of the world's economy has grown, more cultures find themselves driven toward this orientation. Strict schedules bring efficiency. Punctuality is associated with professionalism and respect of the "other." Individualistic cultures, in particular, are most focused on punctuality and a monochronic view of time— defined as doing one thing at a time and segmenting schedules into small precise units. In this orientation, there's a belief that to get things done, one must carefully manage time. Monochromatic cultures view time as a resource similar to money and it is therefore susceptible to being wasted. Most East Asian, North American and Western European cultures tend to be monochromatic (Kaufman-Scarborough & Lindquist, 2016).

"Being" cultures, especially those that are also collectivist in nature, tend toward a much looser, fluid interpretation of time. It's not that time is unimportant in these cultures, rather it's that it is not a resource that can be controlled. Things happen. Schedules and deadlines are based on false assumptions that predictability is possible in all circumstances, the thinking goes. Besides, not everyone deserves our time equally. If a need arises with a family member, this will automatically be prioritized over relationships based on business or friendship. On being late to meetings, people from cultures with this flexible orientation toward time will often offer no excuse, nor will they believe there is a need for one. I once traveled from the United States to Djibouti in East Africa to conduct a two-day leadership seminar for government ministers. After nearly three days of travel I arrived only to find that circumstances had changed. Something had "come up" preventing their attendance. They asked: Could I provide the training the following week or the week after?

This worldview is often referred to as polychronic—defined as a broad, fluid perception of time. In this orientation, people are more committed to relationships than schedules and there's a consistent view that plans are meant to be changed. Most Native American cultures subscribe to this worldview, as do cultures in Latin America, Africa and the Middle East. The Polychronic Attitude Index (Ibid.) was designed to measure preference for polychronicity in four simple statements:

1. "I do not like to juggle several activities at the same time."
2. "People should not try to do many things at once."
3. "When I sit down at my desk, I work on one project at a time."
4. "I am comfortable doing several things at the same time."

This index places individuals on a spectrum from a strong monochronic orientation to a strong polychronic orientation. Travelers from "doing" monochronic cultures often become most frustrated with this aspect of "being" polychronic cultures. Table 2.3 contrasts the two conceptions of time.

### Short-Term vs. Long-Term Orientation

While the "being" vs. "doing" cultural dimension reflects aptitudes about the use of time, short-term vs. long-term orientation reflects

**Table 2.3** The two conceptions of time

| Monochronic Cultures | Polychronic Cultures |
|---|---|
| Do one thing at a time | Do many things at once |
| Concentrate on a task set before them | Concentrate on an event happening around them |
| Consider time commitments (deadlines, schedules) seriously | Consider objectives (goals, results) seriously |
| Are low-context and need information | Are high-context and already have information |
| Are committed to the job and end results | Are committed to people and relationships |
| Dedicate themselves to plans | Change plans often and easily |
| Are more concerned with privacy and individual ownership | Are more concerned with community and shared connections |
| Emphasize prompt time recognition, regardless of relationship or circumstances | Emphasize response based on nature of relationship and circumstances |
| Have strong tendency to build temporary, practical relationships | Have strong tendency to build lifetime, familial relationships |

Adapted from Carol Kaufman-Scarborough's "Two Perspectives on the Tyranny of Time," *The Journal of American Culture*, 2003, pp. 87–95.

aptitudes on the very nature of time. Cultures with short-term orientation are also referred to as "pragmatic" cultures, in that they tend to maintain their traditions and view change with suspicion. Much of the developing world falls into this category, but Anglo cultures also share short-term tendencies. Savings rates in countries with this orientation tend to be much lower and people often make decisions based on factors that lead to quick results. These pragmatic cultures are also more competitive, market-driven and results-oriented (Hofstede, 1994).

Cultures with long-term orientation emphasize the possibilities of the future and tend to adapt and encourage innovation. There is far less concern for tradition. People from these cultures are better at persevering in the case of economic or social setbacks. Long-term cultures have the quality of patience and focus on long-term, even generational rewards. Confucian cultures such as China and South Korea are examples of cultures with a long-term orientation.

In the study of intercultural communication, one of the more popular frameworks used to understand cultural differences is the continuum of context, or larger meaning derived from communication. Low-context cultures prefer direct verbal communication. People tend to be direct and explicit. Communication is intended to leave little to subjective interpretation. In low-context cultures, misunderstandings are considered to be the fault of the communicator. Something that was said was not clear or detailed enough to convey meaning. Therefore, great emphasis is given to verbal skill development in low-context cultures. Educational institutions spend a great deal of effort on verbal communication skills that ensure clarity and effectiveness (Hall, 1973).

High-context cultures, on the other hand, emphasize non-verbals. The environment plays a role in the communication process and the listener pays as close attention to what is not said as to what is said. Appearance matters. Interestingly, failures in communication are presumed to be the fault of the listener. High-context cultures also tend to be collectivist and rely on interpersonal relationships to substitute for more direct conversational styles. For this reason, high-context cultures can be very difficult for outsiders. The classic description of a high-context culture can be found in an outsider asking for directions from a local. The local makes many assumptions and refers to physical features no longer there, ownership of land that an outsider couldn't possibly know and other references that confound and confuse. The low-context traveler just wants to know where to turn left and right.

This continuum can best be understood by considering difference in styles between direct vs. indirect communication. One of the more interesting expressions of indirect communication is the concept of double-voiced discourse, or heteroglossia (Bakhtin, cited in Morris, 1963: 102–111). In this manner of communicating, the speaker anticipates the listener's interests and perspective and adjusts to take in the counterpart's views and concerns. It involves an awareness and respect for others engaged in the dialogue. This way of communicating may have trends that span all cultures. For example, researchers have found that women are four times more likely to use double-voiced discourse than men (Baxter, 2014). Researchers have also found this to be a common practice of minority cultures within larger, dominant cultural settings (Ball & Warshauer Freedman, 2004).

All of this is in in direct opposition to single-voiced discourse, in which the speaker communicates in a linear, straightforward way. In high-context settings, single-voiced discourse can appear blunt and even rude. The same can be said of low power distance societies, so care must be taken to understand the broader expectations of every participant in the conversation.

### Neutral vs. Affective Expression

Cultural orientation has a significant impact on what is considered appropriate in terms of the display of emotion while communicating. Neutral cultures encourage calm and control. They stay focused on the facts at hand and rarely venture into the causal factors of disagreement or disaster. The United Kingdom's cultural reputation for maintaining a "stiff upper lip" and to "keep calm and carry on" is an expression of the values of a neutral culture. Germany, the Nordic countries and Anglo cultures generally are predominantly neutral. Asian cultures, particularly Japan, tend to be neutral. Silent reactions to events are normally seen as a sign of respect and forbearance.

Affective cultures allow for the free, open and spontaneous expression of emotion. They encourage openly passionate reactions to events. Silent reaction to a natural disaster, for example, is viewed as awkward and inappropriate, while emotive expressiveness is expected. Italy, France, Spain and Latin American cultures are examples of affective cultures. There is a tendency toward dramatic facial expressions, gesturing and loud expressions from people brought up in affective cultures. When traveling from an affective culture to a neutral one, care must be taken to take cues from the host culture. People traveling from neutral to affective cultures can seem standoffish and dour.

### Particularism vs. Universalism

Particularism can be defined as the belief that circumstances dictate how ideas and practices should be applied, while universalism is the belief in a singular reality and that ideas and practices everywhere apply evenly. Particularists believe every situation and relationship is different and should be handled as such. Universalists focus on formal rules to guide behavior and belief in all circumstances (Hampden-Turner, 1997). This cultural dimension defines the lens through which to see personal obligation to standards, rules and laws. It is Exhibit A in the case against the creation of binding international law. The continuum representing this dimension is quite broad. Consensus on the appropriateness of definitions of corruption, bribery and fairness is nearly impossible to reach.

Those living in universalist cultures such as those found in the United States, Western Europe, Australia and Canada tend to be very judgmental of particularist countries. They often see cultures driven by *baksheesh* (a small sum of money given as a tip, bribe or charitable donation), for example, as being inherently corrupt. Alternatively, particularist cultures like those found in Russia, the Middle East, and Latin America view universalist claims as hypocritical, naïve, or even unjust. Relationships are dynamic. Situations evolve. There can be no accounting for every possibility with codified rules, so why bother? Particularist cultures are built on a complex web of relationships and circumstances.

### APPLYING CULTURAL COMPETENCE IN LEADERSHIP

Hofstede's research, the GLOBE Study, and countless other cross-cultural projects have sought to provide a lens through which to see cultural differences and similarities more accurately. The wise leader, much like the wise traveler, will be aware of these lenses and employ them in every interaction. One cannot direct, influence and inspire others without understanding their expectations and orientation on fundamental matters pertaining to behavior and values. As self-help guru Stephen Covey (1989) once proposed in *The 7 Habits of Highly Effective People*: Seek first to understand, then be understood. Successfully directing, influencing and inspiring demands contextual expertise in broad belief systems, which is difficult enough when working within one's own culture, given the need to differentiate between individuals. But at least we can assume trends of expectations regarding beliefs and values. When working in a culture foreign to our own, group tendencies must first be mastered. Awareness of the many cultural dimensions is a great place to start.

**TAKEAWAYS FOR THE LEADER IN APPLYING CULTURAL COMPETENCE**

If cross-cultural competence is an important skill for leaders at all levels, then understanding dimensions of cultural value is the starting point. Carefully observing where a culture stands on the following scales leads to greater awareness and understanding:

- Low vs. High Power Distance
- Low vs. High Uncertainty Avoidance
- Individual vs. Collective Identity
- Cooperative vs. Competitive
- Being vs. Doing
- Short-Term vs. Long-Term Orientation
- Direct vs. Indirect Communication
- Particularism vs. Universalism
- Neutral vs. Affective Expression.

**CULTURAL AWARENESS SELF-ASSESSMENT**

1. Am I aware of the norms associated with my own culture regarding the dimensions of cultural value?
2. Which differences in dimensions of cultural value make it most difficult to me to understand or assimilate within another culture?
3. What lessons from observed differences in dimensions of cultural value can I take with me to become a better leader?

**NOTE**

1 Referred to as the Culturally Endorsed Implicit Theory of Leadership or CLT (House et al., 2004).

**ADDITIONAL RESOURCES**

Hofstede, G. H. (1980). *Culture's consequences: International differences in work-related values.* Thousand Oaks, CA: Sage (revised and expanded in 2001).

Chhokar, J. S. Brodbeck, F. C., & House, R. J. et al. (Eds.) (2007). *Culture and leadership across the world: The GLOBE book of in-depth studies of 25 societies.* Mahwah, NJ: Lawrence Erlbaum.

Inglehart, R. (1997). *Modernization and post-modernization: Cultural, economic, and political change in 43 societies.* Princeton, NJ: Princeton University Press.

Ronen, S., & Shenkar, O. (1985). Clustering countries on attitudinal dimensions: A review and synthesis. *Academy of Management Review,* 10(3), 435–454.

Schwartz, S. H. (1994). Beyond individualism/collectivism: New cultural dimensions of values. In U. Kim, H. C. Triandis, Ç. Kâğitçibaşi, S.-C. Choi, & G. Yoon (Eds.), *Individualism and collectivism: Theory, methods, and applications*. Thousand Oaks, CA: Sage.

Schwartz, S. H. (1999). A theory of cultural values and some implications for work. *Applied Psychology*, 48(1), 23–47.

Smith, P. B., & Peterson, M. F. (1995). Beyond value comparisons: Sources used to give meaning to management work events in twenty-nine countries. Paper presented at the annual meeting of the Academy of Management, Vancouver, Canada, August 1995.

## REFERENCES

Ball, A., & Warshauer Freedman, S. (2004). *Bakhtinian perspectives on language, literacy and learning*. London: Cambridge University Press.

Baxter, J. (2014). *Double-voicing at work: Power, gender and linguistic expertise*. London: Palgrave McMillan.

Covey, S. R. (1989). The seven habits of highly effective people: Restoring the character ethic, New York, NY: Simon & Schuster.

Hall, E. T. (1973). *The silent language*. New York, NY: Random House.

Hofstede, G. (1991). *Cultures and organizations: Software of the mind*. London: McGraw-Hill.

Hofstede, G. (1994). *Uncommon sense about organizations: Cases, studies and field observations*. Thousand Oaks, CA: Sage.

House R. J. et al. (Eds.) (2004). *Culture, leadership, and organizations: The GLOBE Study of 62 societies*. Thousand Oaks, CA: Sage.

Hampden-Turner, C., & Trompenaers, F. (1997). *Riding the waves of culture: Understanding cultural diversity in business*. London: Nicholas Brealey.

Inglehart, R. (1997). *Modernization and post-modernization: Cultural, economic, and political change in 43 societies*. Princeton, NJ: Princeton University Press.

Iyengar, S. S., & Lepper, M. R. (1999). Rethinking the value of choice: A cultural perspective on intrinsic motivation. *Journal of Personality and Social Psychology*, 76, 349–366.

Katz, L. (2014). *The global business culture guide: Hints and caveats for doing business in 50 countries around the world*. Charleston, SC: CreatSpace.

Kaufman-Scarborough, C. (2003). Two perspectives on the tyranny of time. *The Journal of American Culture*, 26(1), 87–95.

Kaufman-Scarborough, J. D., & Lindquist, C. (2016). The polychronic-monochronic tendency model: PMTS scale development and validation. *Time and Society*, 16(2–3), 253–285.

Morris, P. (1963). *The Bakhtin reader*. London: Edward Arnold.

Ronen, S., & Shenkar, O. (1985). Clustering countries on attitudinal dimensions: A review and synthesis. *Academy of Management Review*, 10(3), 435–454.

# Three

JOSEPH J. THOMAS

## EXPERIENTIAL LEARNING

American psychologist and philosopher John Dewey (1859–1952) had a tremendously broad range of interests, ranging from aesthetics to social theory. Pragmatic and deeply committed to civil society, he is considered a founder of functional psychology (Shook, 1998). Dewey's greatest influence, however, was on the field of education. His "laboratory school" affiliated with the University of Chicago led him to publish *Democracy and Education* (1916), but it was his master work, *Experience and Education* (1938a), published 20 years later, that has had the most enduring impact on the field of education.

In a mere 91 pages, *Experience and Education* lays the groundwork for the future of education by differentiating traditional and progressive education. Dewey defines traditional as a static approach that emphasizes stillness, quiet and conformity. Educators dogmatically communicate knowledge and skills and strictly enforce rules of conduct. Learners passively commit lessons to memory and obey. In progressive education, Dewey argues, learners must first be given a sense of purpose. Educators create conditions where the learner observes objective conditions, assesses the situation, compares it to past experience, and uses judgment as well as memory to determine significance. The learner makes meaning by grounding unfamiliar concepts with other aspects of known life experience (Dewey, 1938b).

Dewey argues that not all experiences are created equal. They must be organized to create continuity and connections to increasingly significant meaning. Dewey refers to this concept as the "experiential continuum." When arranged correctly, experiences "arouse curiosity, strengthen initiative, and set up desires and purposes" that carry learners through challenging or slow times. Educators must acknowledge that all experience is ultimately social and involves contact and communication (Dewey, 1938a).

DOI: 10.4324/9781003213352-4

By the 1970s, researchers such as David A. Kolb and Ron Fry of the Weatherhead School of Management at Case Western Reserve University began to formalize Dewey's beliefs about progressive education in a general theory of experiential learning (Fry, 1975). Their Experiential Learning Model was comprised of four elements: concrete experience, observation of and reflection on that experience, formation of abstract concepts based on that reflection, and testing the new concepts. These four elements create a spiral of learning, typically beginning with concrete experience, that should be repeated throughout an educative experience.

Experiential learning as a discipline within the larger field of leader development and education has been making great strides in the past decade. This fact is in direct parallel with my personal experience. My own path in leader development began in the mid-1990s, with assessing existing leadership curriculum. The leadership classroom was the venue and traditional statistical assessment was the tool for evaluating success. I later moved on to developing and teaching leadership curriculum in that same classroom environment and evaluating

# Experiential Learning Process

(Adapted from Kolb 1984)[11]

**Figure 3.1** Experiential learning process

Source: David Kolb as applied by the United States Naval Academy, adapted from Kolb, 1984.

success with those same traditional tools. By 2008, I came to realize that classroom leadership curricula and the traditional means to assess effectiveness are wholly insufficient as leader development. At that point in my career my fundamental professional outlook began to change. I suppose I should have come to that realization a decade earlier, but life's great lessons come slowly and are only crystal clear in hindsight.

My journey into experiential learning started haphazardly. I pursued "skipper" qualification on the sailboats that my Naval Academy students use to learn the technical skills of seamanship and boat handling, as well as small unit leadership skills in challenging environments (no small leap for me as a landlubber with only limited "seagoing" experience). I moved into more familiar territory when I became qualified as a hiking/backpacking instructor for the National Outdoor Leadership School (NOLS) in Lander, Wyoming. For years my students had reported "life-changing" summer leadership experiences from NOLS courses in Alaska, Wyoming, the Yukon and elsewhere. I felt a need to experience it firsthand and became convinced that the classroom of backcountry wilderness, like the open sea in a small boat, was more than a curious diversion in leader development curricula. Learning environments that provide immediate consequences to plans, decisions and actions are a necessity. I began to incorporate other experiential learning activities into my routine, such as Staff Rides—walking tours of battlefields to place students in the footsteps of commanders whose plans, decisions and actions could only be fully appreciated by seeing what was experienced. One such Staff Ride involved a nearly 100-mile hike to gain an appreciation for the challenges of General Stonewall Jackson's "foot cavalry" during the 1862 Shenandoah Valley Campaign. I continue to build outreach experiences with organizations such as Outward Bound in order to push the boundaries of the leader development experience at my institution.

It can be said that I am late in joining the party and that there's little new in my attempt to broaden leader development. I know of individuals and institutions that have staked their very identity on this approach and are doing tremendous work to expand and validate the field. However, I have not seen many who have mastered both parts of this equation—well-developed leadership curricula (classroom) rooted in the social *and* behavioral sciences and a fully integrated experiential component to complement the classroom in very deliberate ways. Some have a classroom component *par excellence* while having only nominal experiential programs. Others have epic experiential programs unsupported by a rigorous classroom curriculum. The proper balance is difficult to achieve and varies according to institutional objectives. So, what is generally the best balance between classroom instruction in leadership and reinforcing experiences—and what is the most effective means to measure success? The answers may be simpler than one might imagine.

### DETERMINING THE MOST APPROPRIATE LEADERSHIP CURRICULUM

While there are countless undergraduate and graduate leadership courses and a growing number of major/minor/degree/specialization/certification offerings at both levels, the number of coherent, validated programs is relatively small. It's been said that leader development is a "growth industry" in higher education, but like other industries in their infancy, it is barely coherent. What passes for leadership curricula is often an ill-conceived conglomeration of management, behavioral science and philosophy courses loosely linked together by vague learning outcomes. Assessment of those outcomes is rarely attempted. Good programs map institutional learning outcomes (aren't all universities and colleges in the business of building leaders today?) to departmental or even course objectives. Instructors then map those departmental or course objectives to assessment rubrics and even individual exam questions. Great programs are able to demonstrate emphasis on specified elements of leader development (e.g. critical thinking, decision-making, emotional intelligence, communication skills, etc.) across the curricula.

What are the components of a solid leadership curriculum? The possibilities are endless but a few essentials include:

- Ethics, character, and moral responsibility
- Decision theory
- Effective communication
- Leadership theory (e.g. trait, style, and situational approach; contingency, path-goal, and leader–member exchange theory; and transformational, psychodynamic and servant leadership approach)

- Fundamentals of applied behavioral and social science (e.g. social psychology, organizational psychology, culture and conflict theory, and cognitive science)
- Fundamentals of applied humanities (e.g. practical, context archives, appropriate historical case studies, logic, and applied philosophy).

The scope and intensity of such broad curricula is determined by time available and educational outcomes desired. There are nearly 200 graduate and undergraduate programs in leadership in the United States alone. There are countless leader development programs in the private sector and dozens of leadership institutes and research centers. Models exist for virtually any institutional need or goal.

## DETERMINING THE MOST COMPLEMENTARY EXPERIENTIAL PROGRAMS

Experiential learning is not for everyone. Universities and corporate training offices can offer a stimulating classroom environment to their students while at the same time offering excellent internships, study abroad opportunities, physically demanding practicums and other options that can be rightfully called Experiential Leader Development without explicitly tying the two learning environments together. However, by not tying the two together with unifying language, complementary outcomes, and reinforcing assessment, a hollow program is generally the consequence. Linking the two elements of leader development is hard, time-consuming work. Above all, it demands close collaboration between all faculty and staff across the enterprise.

For most colleges, universities or corporate learning organizations, this effort is best represented in a five-year (at minimum) continuum. The process should begin with a simple identification of institutional outcomes and a translation of those outcomes into practicable learning objectives. These objectives can be the basis of curriculum development, if none currently exists, or curriculum coordination, where mature programs are in place. There are several vital elements of experiential learning:

- Consequences are the first and most important element of experiential learning. They can be of a physical nature, involve professional reputation or pride, or monetary reward (often least effective).

- Commitment to organizational, as well as personal, gain is essential.
- "Epic": Appeal. Participants must be convinced that this is worthwhile, exciting, rewarding, and non-trivial.
- Unique: The more the event appears to be tailor-made to the organization and individuals involved, the more participant enthusiasm is generated.

### THE STATES OF KNOWING AND OF BEING

The U.S. Military Academy at West Point provides a brilliantly simple framework for considering leader development programs: KNOW/DO/BE. Simply put, there are things that must be learned through traditional classroom and practical applications (KNOW). Skills and abilities must be exercised and the associated psychomotor applications assessed (DO). Finally, embodiment of values and qualities that underpin the definition of leadership is required (BE). It is this last point that is most difficult to define and assess. There are four states of being that, I believe, characterize classical attributes of well-rounded leaders. One only achieves these states through careful and thorough preparation.

- **Competence** can be defined in a number of ways—from the simple "do well in your primary field" to the current model of knowledge, skills, abilities, and aptitude (KSAA) that is popular in the public sector. Assessing knowledge is straightforward. Measuring skills and abilities can be more complex. Measuring aptitude is difficult, particularly with self-reporting instruments. There will be more on specific assessment instruments and procedures in a later discussion.
- **Ataraxia (Ἀταραξία)** is a Greek term typically associated with the Stoic philosophers and is generally interpreted as a state free of worry or preoccupation with that which is unimportant or beyond one's control. For contemporary leaders, achieving *Ataraxia* means being cool under pressure, focused on that which is truly important and above petty or selfish squabbling. Assessing such an attribute is typically limited to guided observation from an experienced and vetted observer.
- **Virtus** is the Roman conception of character, originally derived from the ideal "manly" virtues of valor, honor and moral rectitude.

Today we interpret it as those qualities of character that determine one to be fit for the public role of leadership—or placing the common interest and that of the organization one serves above one's own interest. When *virtus* approaches perfection, one achieves a state of *arete* (ἀρετή), or living up to one's full potential. There are many assessment tools that identify predispositions or qualities of character. Examples include Values in Action (VIA), elements of the Multi-Institutional Study of Leadership (MSL), or InfoMart's Character Assessment.

- **Intellectually curious** is the fourth and final state of being that will guarantee growth, adaptability and continuous improvement. While many consider intellectual curiosity to be innate, it can be enhanced: It is the shared responsibility of the individual and the learning organization. Schools and training organizations can incentivize such curiosity by rewarding accomplishment of educational objectives. Selecting the appropriate incentive can be tricky work. Encouraging intrinsic motivation to learn is obviously the best method, but that method is rarely obvious. Perhaps the best encouragement is the design and delivery of engaging material.

There are many other states of being generally considered essential to leadership. However, these four collectively represent a quality, when found in an individual, that will transform organizations and individuals making up those organizations. Building programs to address the cognitive, affective and psychomotor domains of learners demands resources. Decisions to invest heavily in such programs are rarely simple. In conclusion, great leader development programs are the product of focused curricula, complementary experiences and sound assessment. There is no shortcut to such programs. They are labor intensive and require near-constant revision. When done correctly, however, such programs deliver on lofty outcomes.

### EXPERIENTIAL LEADERSHIP DEVELOPMENT (ELD)

Experiential Leadership Development (ELD) involves the integration of classroom instruction and experiential activities in an experiential learning cycle, wherein individuals make meaning of an experience through reflection and contextualization, and then experiment with new approaches or techniques to effect different outcomes in future experiences. Students encounter numerous experiential learning opportunities during a typical four-year college experience, ranging from their daily interaction with peers and faculty in a structured, hierarchical environment, to summer internships and development experiences. However, for these activities to contribute most effectively to ELD, they must incorporate three distinct pillars: risk, responsibility, and reflection.

ELD programs and activities involve the learner taking on some form of risk. At the extreme, this can involve risk of physical injury or damage to equipment, but more often it simply involves risk of failure—to complete a task, achieve a goal, or perform to their own or someone else's expectations. Facing these risks and overcoming the uncertainty, discomfort, or fear inherent in doing so not only strengthens a learner's character, but also heightens the intensity of the learning experience, tapping into emotional responses that make the experience—and its lessons—more memorable and meaningful.

Acceptance of risk is often linked to acceptance of *responsibility*. Taking responsibility for achieving outcomes, particularly when leading others, inherently involves taking risk, and can test a learner's moral courage, wisdom and self-control. Learners often avoid stepping up to take responsibility among their peers, so ELD activities are intentionally designed to give individual learners responsibility and to hold them accountable to fulfill that responsibility.

*Reflection* transforms the experience into practical knowledge that can be applied to future endeavors. Guided reflection—using prompts from seniors, mentors or supervisors and captured in a format for future use—encourages learners to analyze and assess the causes and effects of their successes and failures, and then to use this introspection to set new goals for their own personal development. The most effective ELD activities use reflection *before* the experience to get learners to think about what they want to achieve during the experience, what knowledge gained from the classroom or previous experiences they bring into the activity and what they expect to learn from it. Then, effective ELD programs follow the activity with an additional reflection activity designed to capture the lessons learned and generalize them to other leadership scenarios. Only through this kind of careful reflection can learners effectively gain meaningful, applicable knowledge and wisdom from the experience.

## IMMERSIVE ENVIRONMENTS: STUDY ABROAD AS
## LEADER DEVELOPMENT

Cross-cultural competence is not easily achieved, even through immersive experience in foreign cultures. I have come to realize there are few, if any, programs that combine risk, responsibility and reflection in a deliberate way. In all three pillars the classroom alone is wholly insufficient preparation for practitioners. Internships, practical immersions and study abroad programs by themselves are equally insufficient. However, most would agree that globally aware, ethical leaders hold the key to success in business, philanthropy, politics, security and education. The combination of these three pillars, therefore, represents a critical opportunity in higher education.

Building meaningful collaborations across departments and disciplines is difficult and seldom attempted. Since many colleges and universities don't have specific departments of leadership or ethics, and few have a singular focus on a cross-cultural competence learning outcome, imagination is essential. Colleges of business or management typically teach leadership and applied ethics. Philosophy, history and other departments may offer individual courses along these lines. Anthropology, sociology and language studies departments generally offer courses or entire programs designed to build cultural savvy in students. Working collaboratively across the campus can be particularly difficult if there are competing content and pedagogical views.

To capitalize on the challenge to produce globally aware ethical leaders, institutions must try to achieve several aims.

### Build student-centered educative experiences

While the use of the prefix "student-centered" in higher education has become almost cliché, it absolutely applies in this situation. Students must be given great latitude in designing their own program. At minimum, they must have access to a broad variety of topics, teachers and study abroad locations in order to take ownership of their learning experience. In order to do this, the cross-campus collaboration required is extensive.

### Leverage existing courses and programs

Culture, by nearly every measure, is a broad conception. Program designers must begin with an inclusive mindset open to many worldviews. While some institutions may center their efforts on language acquisition or more general anthropological/sociological outcomes, the larger program must assume as interdisciplinary a character as possible. This requires imagination and collegiality.

### The leadership and ethics components must be conscious and initiating rather than contrived and secondary

There's no question there are many acceptable definitions of leadership; however, the institution must clearly define the type and quality of leader it seeks to produce, and explicitly state that the moral component is paramount. At the U.S. Naval Academy, a very carefully considered outcome is explicit in all guiding policy: "leaders of character who are prepared and educated to serve as warriors, standard bearers of the naval profession, and servants of the nation." Each element of that outcome is explained in great detail in policy and mapped in the curricula. An extensive, well supported international program adds cross-cultural competence immersion opportunities in multiple ways. From brief language study abroad trips, to semesters abroad, the International Programs Office builds reflective practice around classroom applications contributed by several departments.

### Obtain resources sufficient to qualify as a "world class" program

Such ambitious undertakings cannot be done cheaply. Faculty and administrator time must be accounted for in classroom and study abroad segments of the program. While students should assume some out-of-pocket burden for their learning, it is critical to identify sustaining quality initiatives early.

### Problems presented to students must be authentic, and consequences of their actions while in the program must be real and understood

It should be made clear that participation is exclusive, even a privilege, driven by student ability and effort. Too many study abroad programs take the shape of an educational vacation. Rigor and challenge are secondary to simple enjoyment. Programs are always more fulfilling when they are highly structured, intense and demanding. Where physical challenge is appropriate and possible, that element should be included as well. (I realize many will disagree on this last point.)

In the end, the program should assess self-awareness, tolerance for uncertainty, and competence. In order to incorporate all three elements, there is a large cognitive component to be addressed *before* the study abroad. Validated diagnostic instruments abound to assist educators. Reflective exercises during the study abroad should, wherever possible, involve guided reflection. Having a faculty member presence in the immersive environment is optimal. Phone and email communication between faculty and student is acceptable. Waiting to collect reflection only at the conclusion of the experience is not acceptable. The post-experience program should be designed to foster intellectual curiosity for further study. All of this takes time and effort. Levels of commitment are typically gauged by the resources dedicated to the program.

## A CASE FOR ENGAGING WITH REMOTE CULTURES
## IN AUSTERE ENVIRONMENTS

I have long believed that succeeding in a world increasingly characterized by volatility, uncertainty, complexity and ambiguity requires both competence and character. Learning enabled by ELD provides unique opportunities to develop both traits in students. While many universities offer study abroad programs, the U.S. Naval Academy has fashioned innovative experiences—Language, Regional Expertise, and Cultural (LREC) immersion, in particular—that complement classroom instruction in numerous ways.

Leadership is an interdisciplinary field that draws upon philosophy, the humanities and behavioral sciences. Learning outcomes drive the competencies we hope to develop in the four-year core curriculum offered at the Naval Academy. Few universities require annual courses in leadership, still fewer have such broad institutional investment in the leadership competence of its graduates. The Naval Academy hires all of its graduates. Regardless of the professional direction our students take, all will assume leadership positions almost immediately upon graduation. The vast majority will lead an incredibly diverse work force in international environments with high stakes consequences. Therefore, standard leadership competencies alone—such as initiative, decisiveness, endurance, compassion and knowledge—are insufficient. The operating environment our graduates face demands cross-cultural competence (3C). We believe 3C provides tools to understand other cultures in a more general, non-specific way, especially differing worldviews, motivations and deeply-held belief systems. When combined with more specific language skills and regional expertise, 3C becomes the foundation for professional success. Its principles can be learned in the classroom, but to be fully developed it must ultimately be practiced in immersive international environments. There is no shortcut to 3C.

Character lessons derived from educative international experiences prove far more useful and lasting than do lessons in competence. Good character entails moral conviction, ethical decision-making and wise judgment. When combined with critical thinking, good character ensures success at a much deeper level. It arms the leader against the most common failing. When leaders fail it is far, far more common to fail as a result of moral, rather than technical, mistakes. Cross-cultural immersion helps us hold a mirror to our own belief systems while examining those of others. We are forced to confront how we make decisions. We are forced to question our most deeply-held values. Such self-examination is a prerequisite of character development. Such reflection is enabled by exposure to strange and uncomfortable settings.

My personal interest in cross-cultural competence and character development brings me to a few important conclusions. Among them is my belief that engagement with remote cultures in austere environments is the most immediate path to life-changing experiences. The more dissimilar the culture and environment from your own, the more opportunity there is to learn. My choice in Language, Regional Expertise and Cultural Awareness immersions (LRECs) over the past 11 years has been driven by this belief. My students and I have engaged with the Zulu in South Africa, Bedouin in Jordan, Hmong in Vietnam, Kurds in Turkey, Tibetans in China, nomadic herders in Mongolia, Berber in Morocco, Quechan in Peru and the Zanskari in India, among others. We've had to hike, paddle and even ride camels to meet and live among these peoples.

Not every educator will have opportunities to immerse learners in such exotic experiences, but with a little imagination and a coherent plan, anyone can combine Experiential Leader Development with immersive study abroad to create life-changing opportunities.

## TAKEAWAYS FOR EDUCATORS IN EXPERIENTIAL LEADER DEVELOPMENT

The following checklist can guide the development of ELD programming:

How to develop[1] leadership.[2]

- Determine organizational and personal needs (through personal surveys and interviews).
- Determine organizational and personal outcomes.[3]
- Have a conversation to determine values, principles, identity.
- Have a conversation to determine mental models[4] and biases.[5]
- Discuss themes for improvement (plan).
- Discuss commitment requirements for improvement plan.
- Execute plan.
- Obtain feedback on progress and measure success.

Repeat

### NOTES

1 *Develop*—A combination of coaching, mentoring, educating and training for performance improvement.
2 *Leadership*—The process of inspiring, influencing or directing the efforts of others to a common purpose.
3 (for example) *Critical thinking*—Solving problems in the presence of past precedent, experience, procedures or rules. *Creative thinking*—Solving problems in the absence of past precedent, experience, procedures or rules.
4 *Mental Model*—A simple concept to explain complex phenomena.
5 *Bias*—An obstacle to effective thinking.

### ADDITIONAL RESOURCES

Anderson, D. W., Krajewski, H. T., Goffin, R. D., & Jackson, D. N. (2008). A leadership self-efficacy taxonomy and its relation to effective leadership. *The Leadership Quarterly*, 19, 595–608.
Bandura, A. (1997). *Self-efficacy: The experience of control*. Basingstoke: Macmillan.
Dewey, J. (2016). *Democracy & education*. Chicago, IL: University of Chicago.

Eich, D. (2008). A grounded theory of high-quality leadership programs: Perspectives from student leadership development programs in higher education. *Journal of Leadership & Organizational Studies*, 15, 176–187.

Ewert, A., & Sibthorp, J. (2009). Creating outcomes through experiential education: The challenge of confounding variables. *Journal of Experiential Education*, 31(3), 376–389.

Hannah, S. T., Avolio, B. J., Luthans, F., & Harms, P. D. (2008). Leadership efficacy: Review and future directions. *The Leadership Quarterly*, 19, 669–692.

Hiller, N. J. (2005). An examination of leadership beliefs and leadership self-identity: Constructs, correlates, and outcomes. (Unpublished doctoral dissertation). Pennsylvania State University, University Park, PA.

Hughes, R. L., Ginnet, R. C., & Curphy, G. J. (2010). *Leadership: Enhancing the lessons of experience* (7th ed.). New York, NY: McGraw-Hill/Irwin.

Markus, H. (1977). Self-schemata and processing information about the self. *Journal of Personality and Social Psychology*, 35(2), 63–78.

Markus, H., Cross, S. E., & Wurf, E. (1990). The role of the self-system in competence. In R. J. Sternberg & J. Kolligian, Jr. (Eds.), *Competence considered* (pp. 205–226). New Haven, CT: Yale University Press.

McCall, M. W. (2010). Recasting leadership development. *Industrial and Organizational Psychology*, 3, 3–19.

McKenzie, M. D. (2000). How are adventure education program outcomes achieved?: A review of the literature. *Australian Journal of Outdoor Education*, 5(1), 19–28.

McKenzie, M. (2003). Beyond "the outward bound process": Rethinking student learning. *Journal of Experiential Education*, 26(1), 8–23.

Merton, R. K. (1948). The self-fulfilling prophecy. *The Antioch Review*, 8(2), 193–210.

Nadler, R. S. (1993). Therapeutic process of change. In M. A. Gass (Ed.) *Adventure therapy: Therapeutic applications of adventure programming* (pp. 57–69). Dubuque, IA: Kendall/Hunt.

Neves, P. (2012). Organizational cynicism: Spillover effects on supervisor subordinate relationships and performance. *The Leadership Quarterly*, 23(5), 965–976.

Pedhazur, E. J., & Schmelkin, L. P. (1991). *Measurement, design, and analysis: An integrated approach*. Hillsdale, NJ: Lawrence Erlbaum Associates, pp 482–492.

Seibert, K. W., & Daudelin, M. W. (1999). *The role of reflection in managerial learning: Theory, research, and practice*. Westport, CT: Quorum Books.

Shook, J. R. (1998). Wilhelm Wundt's contribution to John Dewy's functional psychology, *Journal of the History of the Behavioral Sciences*, 31, 347–369.

Sibthorp, J. (2003). An empirical look at Walsh and Golins' adventure education process model: Relationships between antecedent factors, perceptions of characteristics of an adventure education experience, and changes in self-efficacy. *Journal of Leisure Research*, 35(1), 80–100.

Walsh, V., & Golins, G. (1976). *The exploration of the outward bound process*. Denver, CO: Colorado Outward Bound School.

Wojcikiewicz, S. K., & Mural, Z. B. (2010). A Deweyian framework for youth development in experiential education: Perspectives from sail training and sailing instruction. *Journal of Experiential Education*, 33(2), 105–119.

## REFERENCES

Dewey, J. (1938a). *Experience and education*. West Lafayette, IN: Kappa Delta Pi.

Dewey, J. (1938b). *Logic: The theory of inquiry*. New York, NY: Holt, Rinehart, & Winston.

Fry, R., & Kolb, D. A. (1975). Toward an applied theory of experiential learning in C. Cooper (Ed.), *Theories of Group Process*. London: John Wiley & Sons.

Kolb, D. A. (1984). *Experiential learning: Experience as the source of learning and development*. Englewood Cliffs, NJ: Prentice-Hall.

# Four

Clementine K. Fujimura

## INTRODUCTION: WHY THE ETHNOGRAPHIC METHOD?

In order to interact effectively and lead in diverse contexts it is imperative that a person become comfortable with experiential learning; that is, that they can notice the differences around them and realize the potential via active engagement and reflection. While this may sound simple, in fact, it does not come naturally to many of us. Engaging means interacting and participating in one's surroundings, consciously shifting perspectives to understand other points of view and being able to navigate and negotiate these differences. Navigating and negotiating requires looking within oneself and analyzing the learning that is taking place.

This chapter begins with an example of perspective-taking and working through differences. This example will lead us to an analysis of the potential of ethnographic methods for leaders. Special attention will be given to an essential component of ethnographies—that of "participant-observation" and its inherent focus on differences in communication styles. By focusing on communication between individuals, a leader can delve more deeply into the nuances of expression and motivations of individuals in any organizational community.

## NAVIGATING VOODOO FOR POSITIVE OUTCOMES

In the following case, we learn about Emily Booth, the creator of Project Fleri, an organization that aims to offer education and community to Haiti's vulnerable children and adolescents. Prior to this project, Booth had visited Haiti after the earthquake in 2010 with her father, an officer in the Air Force, who had been deployed there to help. After her initial experiences in Haiti, she continued to return to support a community called St. Jude. This led her to brainstorm ways that she could make helping the poor in Haiti sustainable. The result was the creation and development of Project Fleri.

DOI: 10.4324/9781003213352-5

While Booth thought herself well prepared because of her years of experience working with children in Haiti, it was not until she found herself leading her dream program that perspective-taking, negotiation and reflection became vital to her continued success. While differences had become apparent during the process of building Project Fleri, at one critical point, she and her host country's cultures actually clashed, as she shares below:

The main goal of my project is to save these boys and girls, so when cultural differences impede our work, we need to use our cumulated experience and knowledge to negotiate.

Such was the case when one boy became terribly sick, vomiting through the night. My first reaction was obviously to take him to the hospital, which we did, but not without a fight. The foster parents in our "welcome home" were convinced that Kesnel, the kid, had a voodoo curse that followed him from his life living with his father, who is a voodoo priest in Jacmel, Haiti. (Before living with his father, who abused him, Kesnel had been a "restavek" [child slave] until the age of 13. He had never been to school.)

After leaving the hospital, Kesnel got sick again the next day and this time I couldn't convince our foster parents that it was just an illness. All of the kids in the house were terrified that the voodoo spirit was going to take over the house so I agreed to go with them up the mountain to visit a priest. Once I was up there, I found out that villagers had already asked an uncle to take Kesnel back in. Apparently, this voodoo curse runs in their family and they know how to deal with it when it comes around.

I was not about to send Kesnel back to a horrible situation he had experienced before moving in with us. After his aunt discovered Kesnel was being horribly abused in his home by his father, the aunt became paranoid of Kesnel's voodoo past and moreover was too poor to pay for his basic needs such as food. She declined to take him in. I could not let him go back to his father, so I called my aunt who is a doctor and had her come up with a logical diagnosis so Kesnel could come back with us to the foster home. She offered the diagnosis of dehydration and, because my American aunt was a doctor (unlike me), our foster parents agreed to let him stay with us.

This was one of the trickiest situations I've had to deal with in Haiti because I didn't want to undermine their beliefs, yet I also knew obviously I had to help Kesnel. I had to respect that Voodoo is their religion and known that I am not going to change their minds. It is something I will always have to work around in Haiti, but also respect.

(Booth, 2020)

As we learn from this case, success in leading the project and realizing its goals by offering the children a home and education required Booth, the leader of the project, to learn the motivations behind behaviors, participate in the community, reflect on why her straightforward approach might not work in the context of Haitian culture, and negotiate with community leaders. While Booth had learned mainly through immersion prior to founding Project Fleri, she was able to hone in on her natural instinct of listening, observing and perspective-taking to achieve her goal in offering another child the opportunity to flourish. If a community of individuals with different cultural backgrounds comes together, success can only be achieved if the leader is willing to step back, allow the differences to be expressed and respected, and negotiate the differences.

## ETHNOGRAPHY AND THE LEADER

The notion of ethnography comes from cultural anthropology—the study of human diversity in societies, with the goal of applying knowledge of cultures to promote cross-cultural understanding. Via ethnographic fieldwork, or simply fieldwork, anthropologists study everyday lives to discover cultural commonalities, what differentiates communities and why people of specific cultures do what they do.

Ethnographic methods and the fieldwork inherent to these methods involve a higher level of experiential learning, which offers a template for effective leadership. Indeed, fieldwork is no longer limited to the realm of cultural anthropology. It is no longer used simply to offer insights about others to others; rather, it is a way for us to learn about each other, ourselves included, and to utilize the deeper learning to communicate and to negotiate constructively and compassionately.

Unlike many quantitative approaches to interpreting others' actions (an etic approach), such as surveys, the ethnographic approach demands that we take an emic perspective: the insider's point of view. While an etic approach, one that observes behaviors from the periphery, is helpful as we gain our point of view as leaders, delving into the emic perspective helps us find meaning in otherwise less understandable behaviors of others. And there's a bonus: Depending on your personality, the emic approach can be fun!

Fundamental to ethnography are the following concepts:

1. Preparation
2. Participant observation
3. Taking notes
4. Reflection
5. Interviews, official and unofficial
6. Communicating our newly acquired depth of understanding (such as in a book, a paper, a film, or simply privately in a journal).

Preparation as leader involves knowing your purpose and, ideally, finding out as much as possible about the individuals on your team before engaging in participant observation. Usually, however, preparation happens as we already find ourselves in a situation that requires us to have learned more about another person's, or group of people's, motivations. Unable to take time to prepare, we need to react and interact while noting the differences among the individuals involved. We might unexpectedly realize that one or more people on our team offer a diverse perspective. Identifying who offers diversity is the first step.

As leaders or teammates, we often do not have time to follow the path of an ethnographer in the preferred order. Rather we adapt and weave in and out of the fundamental concepts. In identifying diversity and differences, we need to take note of what stands out and appears as unfamiliar. How you take note is up to you, but it should involve physical note-taking in some form of writing or voice recording. It does not need to be complicated—whatever works for you, beyond simply making a mental note.

Physical note-taking reminds us of observations we can come back to later as we discover patterns of behavior (or at least develop a deeper understanding of differing values), how people identify themselves (possibly in opposition to how others view them) and the issues at hand. Note-taking also allows us to ask informed questions in formal or even in passing (informal) interviews.

Participation, observation, note-taking and reflection all will help develop perspective-taking and ultimately cross-cultural competence.

## PARTICIPANT OBSERVATION: LANGUAGE AS KEYS TO UNDERSTANDING AND SELF-REFLEXIVITY

Via deliberate and mindful participant observation, we engage with the community, take note of the context and what stands out as unique or interesting, and reflect. It is at the point of reflection that we must also acknowledge our duality: as both an outsider looking in and as a part of the community in which we participate. We become a part of the conversation, affecting, and being affected by, the people involved. A question we need to ask ourselves then is: How is this experience my personal point of view and how much am I changing it by participating and observing? How much is my reflection—my bias? How real and true is my point of view to and for the people I deem to be "different?" What preconceptions do I bring to my participation and observation? Ultimately, we might find partial answers to the question "Who am I?" After all, good leaders are people who have taken the time to learn about themselves as well as those we lead.

Aspects on which to focus our observations include the language people use—both verbal and nonverbal. Which utterances are repeated? A repetition of certain key words or phrases may reflect deeper values or feelings.

In Russian, for example, there are terms that point to the population's continued sense of fatalism. Given Russia's history, it is no surprise that much hope and faith is placed on luck, or, "as luck will have it." Working in Russia, I was reminded daily that outcomes, good or bad, depend in part on the powers of a higher being (only God knows). The term Avos' (авось) is one that underscores the unpredictability that fate will take its course, for good or for bad. I wrote about this in the early 1990s and the idea still prevails:

Avos' (is) more than ambivalence or fatalism. Rather, we come to view it as deeply linked to a feeling of victimization or even "victimhood," as an inevitable experience of Russian life, which entails the experience of *"terpenie"* (patience) and *stradanie* (suffering). However . . . we

> will find that these terms (evoke) a sense of communitas, thereby
> liberating the individual in times of economic and political turmoil.
>
> (Creuziger, 1997: 74–75)

Even in today's social turmoil, this attitude helps motivate particular responses and coping strategies for Russians. As a peer, colleague or leader, knowing this is significant to moving in a desirable direction as a team.

It is easier to gauge the degree to which key words reflect motivation in others than in ourselves. Other people's speech and behavior stands out to us, causing us to ask questions. However, we, too, have key words and idioms that represent deeper values. Some are deeply entrenched, while others develop in popular culture. Take for example the late 2019 term, "Ok boomer." It has come to be used jokingly to undermine someone's ideas or behavior as outdated and similar to that of the uncool baby boomer generation (those born between 1946 and 1964, the postwar time in which there was a baby boom). These individuals referred to as "boomers" tend to be the wealthiest; they have redefined values in the United States. As great consumers, they helped transform economic systems across the world and were generally optimistic about the future and fighting for civil rights and the environment.

That being said, Generation Z, a generation boomers criticize for having "Peter Pan Syndrome" of never growing up, struck back at boomers with "Ok boomer," a term that connotes that boomers, by having too much, went overboard on consumerism, cut taxes, and borrowed money without thinking about the future. When it comes to the environment, while boomers fought openly to save it, little has been done to stop global warming. John F. Kennedy's statement that reflected an ethos of his time—"Ask not what your country can do for you, but what you can do for your country"—was inverted as boomers looked to what they could harvest out of their country:

> This gets flipped on its head in a massive push for privatized gain and
> socialized risk for big banks and financial institutions. This has really
> been the dominant boomer economic theory, and it's poisoned what's
> left of our public institutions.
>
> (Illing, 2017)

Boomers took a lot of what they had for granted, with an emphasis on individual gratification as opposed to sacrifice for the greater good. Author and venture capitalist Bruce Gibney makes clear:

> On an abstract level, I think the worst thing they've done is destroy a sense of social solidarity, a sense of commitment to fellow citizens. That ethos is gone and it's been replaced by a cult of individualism. It's hard to overstate how damaging this is.
>
> (Ibid.)

The term "Ok boomer," while used jokingly in person or online, harbors serious intention. It runs deeper than a slight or witticism. While humorous, it represents a mass subversion, manipulating language, urging boomers to acknowledge their mistakes and to take action. Furthermore, it symbolizes how out of touch the boomer generation is with the conversation between younger generations and, of course, how uncool boomers are. While unknowingly an outsider might mimic and use the phrase, the true meaning demands ethnographic insight.

### NONVERBAL COMMUNICATION

Beyond key words and phrases, the ethnographer must be sensitive to nonverbal language. Some scholars even believe that nonverbal language is more important than verbal language to deciphering meanings. Among the kinds of nonverbal language, there is paralanguage (how the voice communicates) and kinesics (how the body communicates), including facial expression, eye contact, posture, gestures, appearance and proxemics (how we navigate distances between each other).

Let us take paralanguage, for example. It involves vocal qualities such as tone, inflection, volume and/or pitch that we use to change the meaning. Let's compare:

> "How do you solve that equation?" vs. "How DO you solve that equation?!"

Although the words are the same in each, voice emphasis changes the message, revealing emotions and intentions of the speaker. Beyond utilizing this knowledge to understand a team's intentions and emotions, a leader can capitalize on paralanguage to reinforce words, adding to clarity and avoiding conflict. Being self-reflexive on how we use our language, how we subconsciously say things, is helpful in any situation.

Being aware of how individuals or groups of people communicate nonverbally, and using our own nonverbal communication consciously and carefully, is fundamental to strong and effective leadership. Of note for our purposes is being aware of differences in nonverbal communication within a diverse population; it is important to identify and try to understand these differences. Even within the population of a single ethnic group, there may be differences depending on gender, age, and/or religion.

Let us take kinesics and gender in the United States. What is appropriate for sitting in a chair when facing someone else? Most women will keep their legs together either by crossing them or simply placing them closer together, whereas many men find it completely appropriate to keep their knees wide apart. What does this say? In effect, men who naturally sit like this take up more space and dominate the space around them, often causing others to become smaller and to make more room. While this could be analyzed as a negative impact, the tendency for men to sit open-legged in even formal situations is seen as common and it is rarely confronted. Sitting with wide-spread legs in North American culture communicates masculinity and strength. Indeed, it symbolizes the male–female dichotomy in traditional U.S. society in which men tend to have more power than women.

### TAKEAWAYS FOR THE LEADER ON THE ETHNOGRAPHIC METHOD

- Perspective-taking is important for leaders to understand and reap the benefits of diversity.
- In order to understand where individuals of a team are coming from, a leader must engage.
- Engaging requires a conscious decision to interact and observe.
- One can utilize the ethnographic method to formalize the process of engaging.
- Fundamental to the ethnographic method is participant observation, reflection and note-taking.

- Taking note of one's own and others' key words and nonverbal language is essential for positive outcomes.
- As we engage with and support more diversity in North America, we should accept diversity in nonverbal communication and expect to adapt, depending on context.

### SELF-ASSESSMENT ON ETHNOGRAPHIC ACUMEN

1. How do I communicate nonverbally? How do I stand or sit when I talk to people? How do I take up space? How much distance do I prefer to keep when I talk to someone?
2. When was the last time I noticed someone else's nonverbal communication? How do leaders in our society communicate nonverbally and how do I read them?
3. When was the last time I participated in a community or activity that pushed me beyond my comfort zone? How did I respond? Could I have responded better?
4. Are there things that I would like to know more about that would require further study? What are these things? What might knowing more about them do for me in terms of my emerging project?
5. What could I do to engage more with the people I lead or with my peers (professionally and non-professionally)?
6. Are there rules in my workplace that people follow? Are there unspoken understandings? How do people know how to behave? Do different "categories" of people behave differently—young or old, male or female, between ethnic groups, "newbie" or seasoned veteran?
7. What am I doing to ensure that the people I work with are treated respectfully and that I am treated the same way? How do I affect people and how do they behave around me? Sometimes called "reactive effects," these actions can be very revealing. That is, rather than being "bad" because it suggested that you've caused influence (or "contaminated" your site), this becomes a form of data. It can be "good," as long as you don't ignore it, but explore it (Hoey, 2014: 8).
8. What surprises me about the behavior of people at work? Why do I find it surprising?

9. What is my preference for taking note of the things I notice in other people? Can I begin the process right now? (Go grab a journal or notepad and mark it as your observation site/catalog/journal . . . whatever you want to call it, just name it and start!)

## REFERENCES

Creuziger, C. (1997). God's Russian experiment: Hope in the wake of deconstruction of gender and religious identity. *Scholarworks*, Indiana University, pp.75–85. Retrieved from www.Scholarworks.iu.edu

Hoey, B. (2014). A simple introduction to the practice of ethnography and guide to ethnographic fieldnotes. *The Selected Works of Brain A. Hoey*. Huntington, WV: Marshall University.

Illing, S. (2017). How the baby boomers—not millennials—screwed America. Retrieved from www.vox.com/2017/12/20/16772670/baby-boomers-millennials-congress-debt

Interview
Booth, Emily, Spring 2020.

Developing 3C in the Workplace and
the Role of Communication

# Five

CLEMENTINE FUJIMURA

Cross-cultural competence depends on the effort you take to continuously develop understanding, skills, and curiosity in new contexts. Studies have shown that a curious mindset positively influences personal, interpersonal and professional growth. We define curiosity as proposed in Kashdan et al.'s (2004) study on potential for personal growth as "a positive emotional–motivational system associated with the recognition, pursuit, and self-regulation of novel and challenging experiences" (p. 3). Essential to opening the path to curiosity and the ultimate goal of achieving cross-cultural competence is taking the time to deliberately exit your comfort zone—to step out of your normal surroundings into unfamiliar territory. While some professionals might have the time and resources to venture abroad for this development, it is not necessary to go far. Your own country, state, city, or even workplace might very well offer you a venue to advance your cross-cultural competence. That being said, simply going to Chinatown or to an exotic restaurant, while a step in the right direction, is not enough. Approaching an unfamiliar context in a conscious and strategic manner so as to enhance your ability to test yourself and grow is key.

In the following pages, we will explore examples of opportunities for 3C development as well as the necessity of enhancing communications skills. Opportunities can be found in communities nearby or even in the workplace, from nearby campuses to institutional subcultures. However, without the ability to communicate effectively across these communities, 3C will fail.

## OPPORTUNITIES NEXT DOOR

Let's take a walk around Washington D.C., for example. While museums offer historical narratives and artifacts from diverse peoples, they are just the tip of the iceberg. You might also choose to immerse

DOI: 10.4324/9781003213352-6

yourself in coursework at a local university or learn a foreign language. Opportunities abound, with courses at local universities in Chinese, Arabic, Russian—or how about considering American Sign Language (ASL)?

Individuals with their hearing intact might not know of a very important place just off of Florida Avenue in North East Washington, D.C.: Gallaudet University. This university serves the Deaf community and more specifically, has cultivated Deaf culture since 1864. Each year I challenge my students by taking a field trip to this spectacular campus, filled with an oft unknown yet complex network of students and faculty. When I introduce my hearing students from the U.S. Naval Academy, to Gallaudet, they seem pleased: "How nice that we have a university specifically to help people with Deafness as their disability!" they might exclaim. Indeed, via this statement, they have demonstrated their ignorance and potential prejudice. As a teacher of these future Navy and Marine Corps leaders, I feel the need to seize this special opportunity to help them uncover the truth: Deaf culture is not about a disability, but abilities. Gallaudet is a place with a deep history and traditions. It is a place filled with pride in Deaf culture—a culture that many wish to keep alive.

Most individuals seeking to experience a new context might feel a simple walk through the campus would qualify as educational enough to support developing 3C. I would encourage such individuals, yourself perhaps, to do it right: Follow the methods outlined in the chapter on ethnography and begin with preparation, participate and observe, take notes and hold conversations or interviews over an extended period of time. And yes, enrolling in an ASL class might be the perfect means of building relationships and developing your 3C.

Gallaudet University was established to offer a quality education for students with various degrees of deafness. Most interesting in its mission is its support of the Deaf community and Deaf culture. I find that many of my students (perhaps like you, the reader), might not have considered the notion of Deaf culture as a true culture. Instead we assume deafness to be a disability, one that any person would like to "fix." Yet, in our preparation for the field trip, via readings and a few notable films, students learn that Deaf culture is "a set of learned behaviors of a group of people who are deaf and who have their own language (ASL), values, rules, and traditions" (www3.gallaudet.

edu/clerc-center/info-to-go/deaf-culture/american-deaf-culture.
html). Indeed, for many born Deaf (and I capitalize the word so as
to emphasize the cultural component), deafness is something they
would not want to change. Deaf culture includes people who are
proud to be a member of the Deaf community, who see value in
keeping Deaf culture alive to the extent that some members would
rather not have a cochlear implant (a device medically inserted,
designed to mimic hearing and allow for easier communication
with hearing cultures).

It is at this point that students in my class begin to feel discomfort
as they try to adjust to a number of ideas not commonly understood
in hearing cultures: that deafness is not a disability; that Deaf culture
exists and includes all of the elements of hearing cultures, such as
history, language and symbolism; and that people are proud to be
a part of it and that some would prefer it to switching to hearing
cultures.

The assignment is to spend a day (or more) at Gallaudet (we only
have time for day-long field trips, alas); to take a tour and learn about
the institution's history, Deaf architecture and culture; and to speak
with students on the campus and to try to understand Deaf culture
from the members' perspectives and not from students' own biased
views. A final paper will summarize their findings and critiques of
their own explorations. In an amazing turn of events, by the end of
the day, midshipmen return with energy that compels many to return
to Gallaudet, to discover more, to learn ASL, to develop relationships
with the students, and to become advocates of Deaf culture. Some of
my less ambitious academic students often shine in this assignment
and in at least two cases relationships have turned to dates . . . not that
that is the goal! This energy comes from the realization that working
through an uncomfortable moment of culture shock can lead to a new
sense of inner strength and the newly found capability of adaptability.
My students are well on their way to growing their cross-cultural
competence and disassembling their biases.

Indeed, developing cross-cultural competence is a necessary
ingredient to erasing prejudices we hold often subconsciously. When
feasible, I encourage leaders to take the time to approach, interact
with, and explore communities they have found unapproachable
in the past. Perhaps a leader might not have spent a day with the

administrative support staff since rising to the top. There might be people who seek each other out due to similar backgrounds or hobbies in a professional space. Who are the groups of people you see but do not acknowledge?

## DEVELOPING AWARENESS OF CULTURAL BLINDERS

As the leader of a rather large division at one academic institution, Dr. Frederik Delow (not his real name) heard complaints about the rifts people felt between the generations. Young assistant professors enjoyed each other's company, while those with tenure or headed for retirement mixed only with those in their own professional stage. Unable to figure out in his mind what this could all be about, he focused his efforts on enhancing the younger group of professors' experiences and opportunities, as he thought perhaps this was the concern. As a result, he moved his attention away from those he considered stable in their professions and more helpful for organizing committees (considered too time consuming for the assistant professors who need to focus on research and publications for promotion). In a sense, while possibly unaware of this himself, Dr. Delow was demonstrating bias in favor of the new crop of professors.

After a year of this focus on the newer community of scholars, it came to his attention that one of his leading professors, Professor Paul Kim (not his real name), had decided to retire, in part because, as he pointed out, he hoped for more time to conduct research and to write post-retirement. Saddened by the looming loss of Professor Kim, Dr. Delow felt obliged to relieve him from the rigors of some more time-consuming committees during his last year. After all, Dr. Delow wanted Dr. Kim to look back upon his last year with warm feelings. The day came when Dr. Kim was ready to leave and he approached Dr. Delow to bid him a personal farewell: "I just wanted to say a few words before I leave," Dr. Kim began, then continued: "This has been the worst year of my life at the university thanks to your disdain for my work, taking away all my leadership roles on important committees and in effect, putting me out to pasture! I hope no one ever treats you like you treated me!" Without letting Dr. Delow digest the outburst or explain, Dr. Kim left.

In this anecdote, we see that lack of cross-cultural competence is a blinder for Dr. Delow: He does not understand the pre-retirement individuals in his division—that pre-retirement is potentially a time when a person would like to contribute in a meaningful way prior to departure. A lack of such understanding can lead to damaged relationships and a negative work climate. Pre-retirement is a significant time of life in which professionals may leave their long years of service with mixed feelings: on the one hand, happy to delve into something new or still to be accomplished, while on the other hand, feeling a loss of the network of colleagues and professional self-esteem. Dr. Kim wanted to leave knowing he had served and contributed in a meaningful way.

Dr. Delow had not considered that his assumptions about the pre-retirement phase might not apply to everyone. As a concerned leader, he had not taken the time to listen in order to hear different perspectives. Instead, he functioned within the framework of his cultural blinders. No matter what our role at work, we inherently have cultural blinders due to our personal enculturation and socialization that propel us into decisions that are not necessarily in tune with the needs of others. It is up to us to recognize these blinders and to seek ways to remove them.

Had Dr. Delow taken the time to talk to the individual he might have discovered that to Dr. Kim, as to many facing retirement, pre-retirement is an important and potentially evolving (rather than devolving) time. By the time Dr. Delow heard Dr. Kim's concerns, other retirees had probably been made aware of Dr. Delow's insensitivity, lack of support and possible ageism. It might have behooved Dr. Delow to spend time with the various informal social groups in his division, and hear their stories and their concerns, rather than assuming he knew what everyone needed in order to be happy.

Subcultures of an organization, including those defined by professional stage, are important spaces of immersion for a leader. These subcultures include ones that are distinguished by, for example, nationality, ethnicity, gender, hobbies, skillsets, social stratification and lines of expertise or business and professional stage, to name a few. Like culture itself, these subcultures are ever changing. Let's take for example the subculture of professional stage. The stage of pre-retirement was once seen as a stagnant time in one's life—and even one of decline. More recently, however, studies indicate quite the opposite: that pre-retirement and retirement are times when people are realizing and developing new talents, and interests, and even reinventing themselves. According to a number of studies, people often achieve a stronger sense of well-being after leaving their primary profession for retirement (see Dychtwald & Morison, 2020). Moreover, age is not an indicator of activity level, as each individual is different, with many retirees of varying ages seeing retirement as a time of opportunity and personal growth.

Furthermore, not all retirees are alike. There are subcultures within the retiree subculture. For example, there are the "Ageless Explorers" who: "have no intention of winding down. They are most likely to start businesses in retirement or to teach part-time" (Ibid.). While some retirees do wish to take it easy, referred to as the "Comfortably Contents," you might have members of yet another subculture in your division, the "Live for Todays," who seek ongoing reinvention: "These people like challenges and changes . . . they are spontaneous . . . free-spirited, versatile and experimental" (Ibid.). Who works on your team? Do you know their aspirations during and beyond work? Can you take their perspective?

## THE IMPORTANCE OF COMMUNICATION AND CODE-SWITCHING

Taking off our cultural blinders allows us not only to understand different perspectives but to fine-tune our ability to listen and communicate effectively. For not only are we enculturated (both consciously and subconsciously) to become competent in our culture and in our roles within our culture, that is, we internalize the values and expectations of our society, but we are also enculturated to respond in appropriate but culturally limited ways. These "appropriate ways" are contextual and ever-changing. Indeed, learning how to interact even in our own culture is never complete: As we encounter new situations, the skills need to change for effective communication within those situations. As mentioned above, cross-cultural competence involves developing not only understanding and curiosity, but also skills. Culturally appropriate communication is one such skill.

At a small business, two colleagues we will call Janice and Ellen were chosen to coordinate a fundraiser. Janice and Ellen had a few organizational meetings during which they agreed to a plan. After a few days, Janice could be heard complaining that Ellen was slow to get things done and always late for meetings. Janice felt at a loss as to what to do. Ellen on the other hand felt tension and complained that Janice "was intimidating."

Janice had gotten straight to the point, assuming Ellen was ready to jump right in. What intimidated Ellen? Upon further inquiry, it became clear that Ellen was taken aback by Janice's conversational style, which to her seemed abrupt and lacking in sensitivity toward her perspective and ideas. Furthermore, because Ellen was new to the office, she was, as it turns out, waiting for leadership and guidance on exactly how to proceed.

As scholars have pointed out, many of our conflicts are the result of miscommunications, some of which are based on our notions about others, based on their race, gender, ethnicity, disability and/or the meanings behind kinesics (body language) and paralanguage.

Janice's assumption that Ellen would "jump right in" and ignore the fact that Janice had been working in the office longer was problematic. An introductory conversation between the two colleagues, clarifying expectations on their roles, would have paved the way for working together more easily and would also have smoothed the road for their work relationship in general. Lack of verbal communication often leads to misunderstandings.

Ellen feeling intimidated because of Janice's conversational style is something any leader should take note of: How we say things, how we move our bodies, our facial expressions and how we manipulate the sound of language (paralanguage) with tone, volume, and pitch, for example, can be engaging to some and off-putting to others. Does this mean we all need to be concerned about how we speak to others? Well, yes, to some extent. We must be aware of how we present via our communication to various groups of people and be ready to adapt appropriately when necessary. Adapting our language (both verbal and non-verbal) to a particular context is called "code-switching."

Code-switching occurs when there is a need to switch between languages, language variations, dialects and accent, using markers of difference including paralanguage, kinesics or official vs. familial language, for example. These needs occur between genders, hierarchical levels, ethnicities and professions. As Guest points out: "failure to code switch in a communication . . . runs the risk of sending the wrong signals" (Guest, 2020: 108).

Sharpening an ability to switch between styles of communication, learning to think differently as we code-switch (some call this flexing—see Hyun and Lee: 2014) is important when leading and managing people from different walks of life: involving ethnic, gender or even generational differences. Hyun (2014) suggests that a leader consider the perspective of the other person (client, co-worker, junior worker etc.) and solve problems collaboratively and non-confrontationally.

Our personal ability to code-switch needs to be examined and perfected as we develop 3C. How I speak to my doctor is different from how I speak to my close friend. The humor I use with my family in Germany is different from the humor I use with my family in the United States. Some jokes don't fly cross-culturally and in translation. In our example, Janice was possibly unaware that she was being curt and insensitive and may not have fine-tuned the talent of code-switching when talking to new office mates.

In situations of interpersonal conflict in any professional environment, cross-cultural competence of the leadership is imperative. Reaching out, communicating effectively (and often that means sensitively), being curious as to how and why people behave and react the way they do, asking questions, spending time with individuals at various professional levels, adapting and trying to take the other perspective whether or not it is similar to yours, can break barriers, dispel prejudice and ultimately lead to success.

## COMMUNICATION SELF-ASSESSMENT

1. What are the subcultures around me and who might I get to know?
2. When do I code-switch? When should I code-switch?
3. When have I successfully code-switched in the past and what was the result?

## REFERENCES

Dychtwald, K., & Morison, B. (2020). Retirees today: Age isn't a leading indicator, it's a misleading indicator. Forbes, July 13. Retrieved from www.forbes.com/sites/kendychtwald/2020/07/13/retirees-today-age-isnt-a-leading-indicator-its-a-misleading-indicator/#6b6d535d3de0, accessed July 13, 2020.

Guest, K. (2020). *Cultural anthropology: A toolkit for the global age.* New York, NY: W.W. Norton & Company.

Hyun, J., & Lee, A. (2014). *Flex: The new playbook for managing across differences.* New York, NY: HarperCollins.

Kashdan, T. B., Rose, P., & Fincham, F. D. (2004). Curiosity and exploration: Facilitating positive subjective experiences and personal growth opportunities. *Journal of Personality Assessment, 82*(3), 291–305.

# Six

Joseph J. Thomas

International travel offers unrivaled developmental opportunities, but only when the experience is approached with deliberate intent. Learning about new cultures, and also discovering otherwise hidden aspects of one's own culture, are among the more obvious opportunities. The ultimate possibility, however, is to change the very manner in which we see the world, or in other words, to change our thinking. This is every bit as challenging as it is ambitious, but armed with the right tools and techniques, it's achievable. What follows is but a small cross-section of tools and techniques. If used wisely before, during, and after the travel experience, these tools can transform our ability to make better, more timely decisions and more informed judgments. Could there be a better general preparation for leadership? In terms of developing the specific leadership skill of cross-cultural competence, the answer is no.

## DEFINING THE PROBLEM: BIAS

The challenge of biased thinking can adversely impact our day-to-day functioning in the most familiar surroundings. When the complexity and ambiguity of international travel is added to the mix, the challenge is compounded exponentially. There are many ways to define bias, but my personal favorite is among the simplest: "a predictable error that inclines your judgement in a particular direction" (Kahneman et al., 2021). The two key words in this definition that bear particular examination are "predictable" and "error." Predictable implies knowable or even expected. While this may be true for cognitive psychologists or other behavioral scientists, it is rarely true in the context of self-awareness. If this chapter accomplishes anything, I hope it serves as an encouragement to examine our own beliefs, judgments and decision-making. The other word "error" is more open to debate. Error implies problem or even wrongdoing. While this is often the case, biases can

DOI: 10.4324/9781003213352-7

also be value neutral. That is to say, a bias can at times be neither right nor wrong, but rather a simple shortcut in thinking. Such shortcuts are often referred to as heuristics—a more expedient path to ease the cognitive load of decision-making. There will be more on this later in the chapter. For now, we'll focus on bias as error.

In 2016, Buster Benson, a marketing manager at Slack, with the support of illustrator John Manoogian, developed a fascinating tool to better understand the sheer scope of cognitive biases that afflict our decision-making and judgment (see Figure 6.1). While Benson acknowledged the practical nature of biases in saving our brain's time and energy, he also tied diagnosable biases to one of four initiating problems. Each of these four problems is more likely to induce error than not.

The first broad problem that spawns a good number of biases reflects the ever-expanding information environment in which we live. That we have too much information available to us for competent processing is beyond debate. In fact, this phenomenon has come to be called "information shock," as availability of information has

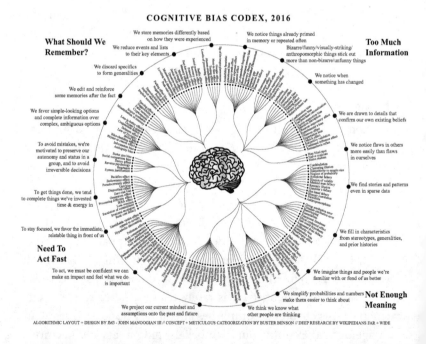

**Figure 6.1** Cognitive bias codex, 2016

Source: B. Benson and J. Manoogian.

dramatically outstripped our capacity to make sense of it. Futurist and systems theorist Buckminster Fuller coined the term "Knowledge Doubling Curve" to describe the rate at which information or "human knowledge" doubles. He posited that until 1900, human knowledge doubled approximately every century. By 1945 knowledge doubling occurred every 25 years. By 2012 knowledge doubled every 13 months and today we are closer to a doubling of information every 12 hours (DellOrgfano, 2020).

In a world characterized by volatility (fast change without a clear predictable trend or pattern), uncertainty (frequently disruptive changes—past is not a predictor of the future), complexity (multiple, interdependent causes) and ambiguity (little clarity about what is "real" or "true"), our capacity to make well-reasoned judgments is limited. Table 6.1 shows some of the cognitive biases driven by having too much information and that are typical when we are immersed in unfamiliar environments and cultures.

**Table 6.1** Cognitive bias—too much info

| | |
|---|---|
| **Availability heuristic** | We overestimate the importance of available information and rely on immediate examples that come to mind when evaluating a topic, concept or decision. |
| **Anchoring bias** | We overly rely on, or anchor, the first piece of information we encounter when making decisions. |
| **Confirmation bias** | We tend to search for, listen to and interpret only that information that confirms our preexisting beliefs. |
| **Ethnocentrism** | We apply our own cultural or ethnic frame of reference to judge the behaviors, beliefs or cultural practices of others unfamiliar to us. |
| **Conservatism bias** | We favor prior evidence or pre-existing information over new evidence that has emerged from direct observation. |
| **Law of triviality** | We typically give disproportionate weight to trivial issues rather than think about complex, challenging phenomena. |
| **Framing effect** | We draw different conclusions from the same information, depending on how that information is presented. |
| **Baader-Meinhoff phenomenon** | We notice things that have been brought to our attention with improbable frequency (also called the Frequency Illusion) |
| **Empathy gap** | We underestimate the strength and influence of feelings that we ourselves and others hold. |

The second problem arises from our inability to make meaning of what we see in the world around us. To save time and energy, the human brain fills in the blanks and creates stories to account for insufficient information. These heuristics help us to simplify probability calculations. When immersed in an unfamiliar culture, individuals often project their mindset onto others. Worse, we falsely assume we know what others are thinking. The more unfamiliar we are with the culture and its people, the more those assumptions will be tinged with a negative framing—or in the immortal lyrics of The Doors' Jim Morrison,

> People are strange when you're a stranger,
> faces look ugly when you're alone,
> women seem wicked when you're unwanted,
> streets are uneven when you're down.
> When you're strange, faces come out of the rain.
> When you're strange, no one remembers your name.

This factor is in large part responsible for my personal belief that the more different the culture is from one's own, the greater the opportunity to learn. My preference has long been remote cultures in austere environments, or as I term them, "cultures writ with a darker pen." I've additionally focused on minority cultures struggling to maintain their cultural identity in the face of majority pressure to do otherwise. Adding physical challenge (e.g. traveling on foot, sleeping on the ground, carrying all necessities on your back, etc.) sets up a learning environment more conducive to open-mindedness and less susceptible to distraction. The result of such immersion, especially as it relates to the development of cross-cultural competence, is to help travelers make sense not only of the culture around them but of their own culture and its role in shaping their system of beliefs. It's for all these reasons and more that understanding meaning-making biases is so important. Of the nearly 200 diagnosed biases found in the Cognitive Bias Codex, the greatest number and widest variety fall under the meaning-making challenge. A small representative sample includes the following:

**Table 6.2** Cognitive bias—meaning making

| | |
|---|---|
| **Stereotyping** | We expect a group or person to have certain qualities without our having a full understanding or reliable information regarding that group or person. |
| **Puritanical bias** | We attribute the cause of an undesirable quality or wrongdoing by a group or individual to a lack of self-control or moral deficiency rather than consider larger environmental determinants. |
| **Bandwagon effect** | We tend to believe things because many other people believe those same things. This is one form of groupthink. |
| **Naïve realism** | We believe we see reality as it really is, objectively and without bias, while others are uniformed, irrational or worse. |
| **Group attribution error** | We believe the decisions, qualities and characteristics of one member of the group are generalizable to all members of the group. |
| **Halo effect** | We perceive a person's positive or negative traits will spill over into other unrelated personality areas. |
| **Not invented here** | We have an aversion to knowledge, products, or standards not developed within our own group or culture. |
| **Just-world hypothesis** | We want to believe the world is fundamentally just and therefore we rationalize the injustice we see as somehow deserved by the victims of that injustice. |
| **Negativity bias** | We recall unpleasant memories much more easily and frequently than positive memories. |

A Chinese proverb states, "An inch of time is an inch of gold, but an inch of gold cannot buy an inch of time." In Western cultures, particularly American culture, an even greater premium is placed on time. We all believe ourselves to labor beneath the tyranny of time. It's the only non-renewable resource. We rarely feel ourselves to have enough time to accomplish important tasks, make informed decisions, or weigh options about the best course of action. This mindset drives us to focus on immediate, relatable things right in front of us. We opt for simple solutions. We prioritize according to what we feel is important or that which we've already invested time and energy in completing. This leads to wholly predictable errors. Some of these decision-making errors include:

**Table 6.3** Cognitive bias—need to act fast

| | |
|---|---|
| **Fundamental attribution error** | We tend to over-ascribe the behavior of others to their innate traits rather than situational factors, leading us to overestimate how consistent that behavior will be in the future. |
| **Influence of stress** | We are made worse by stress. Stress causes both mental and physiological responses and tends to amplify all other biases. Stress causes hasty decisions, immediacy and a fallback to habit. |
| **Dunning-Kruger effect** | There is a tendency for unskilled individuals to overestimate their capability and highly skilled individuals to underestimate their capability. |
| **Reactance** | We feel an urge to do the opposite of what someone wants us to do in order to retain autonomy. |
| **Boredom syndrome** | We have a tendency to act even when action is not required. We also tend to offer solutions when we don't have enough knowledge to solve the problem. |
| **Group- or Self- serving bias** | We tend to evaluate ambiguous information in a way that is most beneficial to our own interests. |
| **Overconfidence effect** | We possess excessive confidence in our own answers to questions. |
| **Hyperbolic discounting** | We have a stronger preference for immediate payoffs rather than more beneficial, long-term payoffs. |

We began our consideration of cognitive biases with a broad category of challenges driven by too much information in our environment. We will conclude by considering a related dynamic: choosing from that information only those elements worth committing to memory. In this process, we discard specifics to form generalities. We reduce lists and events to only their key elements. We store memories differently based on how they were experienced. And finally, we edit and reinforce some memories after the fact. When engaged in international travel and cultural immersion we consciously and subconsciously index the unfamiliar environment in unique ways. The neuroscience of novelty shows we create neural networks that physically remap the brain when engaged in challenging, stimulating activity (Park & Huang, 2010). Few activities are as impactful as international travel.

Activity-dependent plasticity is the reconfiguring and strengthening of the human brain through experiencing new types of cognitive function (Dodge, 2007). It provides evidence for the effectiveness of experiential education, of which immersive international travel is among the most impactful kind. But that impact is only made possible by helping those who experience international travel to codify and index that experience in memories. The many obstacles to doing this effectively include biases as shown in Table 6.4.

Having a general awareness of cognitive biases can make a cultural immersion experience more meaningful. Deliberately reflecting on those biases before, during, and after travel is strongly encouraged. But addressing them in direct response to experiencing them, *in the moment*, is most impactful. Encouraging travelers to journal about the experience is a way to reinforce learning. My challenge to travelers always includes a recommendation to deepen, widen, and lengthen their perspectives. Deepening demands they challenge blind spots and deeply held assumptions or fixed beliefs. Widening requires they address all problems from multiple vantage points and consider multiple perspectives and stakeholders. Lengthening suggests they focus not only on the immediate outcomes of their decisions but on the

**Table 6.4** What should we remember?

| | |
|---|---|
| **Prejudice** | We hold negative feelings about an individual based on our perceptions of their group membership, i.e. race, gender, sexuality, belief system, occupation, wealth, education, age, musical taste, education or some other personal characteristic. |
| **Implicit stereotypes** | We associate particular qualities and social categories to members of a specific group. |
| **von Restorff effect** | We are more likely to remember items, people or experiences that "stick out" or are unique from more similar items, people or experiences. |
| **Negativity bias** | We recall unpleasant memories more readily than pleasant ones. |
| **False memory** | We often mistake imagination for memory. |
| **Google effect** | We forget information that can easily be found in an online search engine. |
| **Cross-race effect** | We have difficulty differentiating individual members of a race other than our own. |
| **Peak-end rule** | We perceive not the sum of the experience but the average of how it was at its peak—whether that peak was pleasant or unpleasant—and how it ended. |
| **Serial position effect** | We remember things best from the end of the trip, followed by things that happened at the beginning. We are least likely to recall things in the middle. |

long-term consequences of their actions (Schwartz, 2018). Bias awareness and perspective-taking are two essential components of cross-cultural competence. Critical thinking skills are the third element to effective problem-solving in a cross-cultural environment.

### DEFINING THE SOLUTION: CRITICAL THINKING

There is no simple solution to biased decision-making, but self-awareness and good critical thinking skills are a start. As with bias, there are many ways to define critical thinking. Some of the earliest definitions and methods date to the time of Socrates. In fact, "Socratic questioning" remains among the best ways to draw out critical

# The Elements of Thought

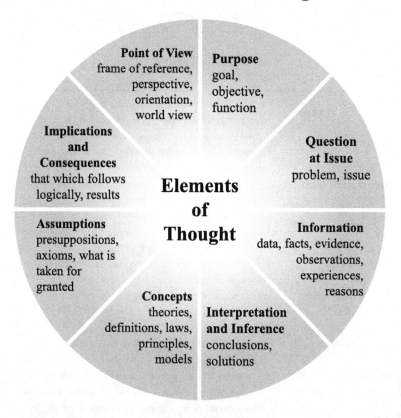

**Figure 6.2** The Elements of Thought

Source: Paul & Elder, *Critical Thinking: Concepts and Tools* (2009).

thinking skills from students—or anyone for that matter. Socrates asked his students to consider verifiable facts before drawing conclusions; he tested the logic of their assumptions and he demanded they apply rigorous standards to their thinking (Taylor, 1989). These techniques are kept alive and well today by organizations such as the Foundation for Critical Thinking (Foundation for Critical Thinking, n.d.). In fact, I have not found a better source of rigorous standards to help travelers think carefully about cultures. I typically begin with Paul and Elder's "The Elements of Thought" (see Figure 6.2).

Keeping a journal is, without question, one of the best practices for drawing the most from cultural immersion experiences. But where to begin? Among the goals for cross-cultural competence is to be consistently fair in our judgments of others. We must use rigorous standards to draw conclusions. Opening the journal with broad questions, often referred to as "prompts," is a great place to start. I suggest the following:

- *What is my purpose for travel? What do I hope to accomplish? What is my primary aim?*

A great next step, and one that would make Socrates himself proud, would be to formulate the most important questions for yourself and others when engaged in travel. These foundational questions might include the following:

- *What questions will I try to answer on this trip? Can major strategic questions be subdivided into smaller tactical questions? What type of judgments will I be required to make in answering these questions?*

As travel commences, journaling should be done daily if possible. I recommend travelers keep their journals close at hand to capture key lessons anytime circumstances allow and that they dedicate at least an hour to journaling each night. This is particularly important for recording observations, experiences, facts, reasons for conclusions and more.

- *What direct observations have I made and what facts have I collected to help me answer the questions I had about this culture? Do I have enough to draw any conclusions?*

Every second or third day, I have a group conversation about our experiences and observations for the purpose of comparing notes. I'm always amazed at how differently two people can see the same situation and draw distinctly different conclusions. By considering the differences in how people experience the same event, travelers refine their thinking and reconsider conclusions. Every fifth or sixth day, I have individual "check-ins" with each traveler and ask them if they've come to any conclusions. I press them to share their conclusions to this point in the trip and add the following prompts to their journals:

- *What conclusions have I made and how did I reach them? How have others interpreted data or facts differently? What inferences have I made to reach my conclusions?*

Most of the cultural immersion trips I have organized and led last about three weeks. This is driven as much by traveler stamina as by resource constraints. Longer trips would be optimal but, in my experience, three weeks is wholly sufficient to accomplish many key outcomes associated with cross-cultural competence. It is usually at the halfway point of the trip (10 or 11 days), then, that I am able to tease out broader concepts and theories the travelers have developed regarding the culture they are experiencing. I ask them to reflect on questions such as:

- *Have you developed any theories about how this culture is different from our own? What makes it similar? What are the best practices for traveling, working and living in this culture that you would share with those who will come after you?*

Asking them to prepare a "traveler's guide" for future travel is a helpful technique to encourage deeper consideration. I'll often ask, "Imagine you're bringing your family here next year; can you prepare a simple guide to help them better navigate the culture? If so, what would it include?" In the last half of the trip we continue to journal daily, meet collectively every two to three days, and check in every fifth or sixth day. During the final check-in, I'll test their ideas for assumptions, implications and point of view. Borrowing again from "The Elements of Thought," I'll ask them to consider:

- *What are you taking for granted? If someone accepted your conclusions about this culture, what would be the implications? Is there another point of view you should consider?*

In the end, I typically find the traveler has reached a point of greater intellectual humility, so that when they conclude that they've come away with more questions than when they started the trip, I can assure them that is a healthy response. We review everything they've seen and learned and then summarize those things they don't know but can explore further, on their own. This intellectual humility is in many ways the bedrock of cross-cultural competence. It prevents all types of bad behaviors associated with socio-centrism and other counterproductive biases.

If "The Elements of Thought" are a useful framework for journaling, then Universal Intellectual Standards are the best tool for ensuring the quality of our thinking and debating about the culture we're experiencing. These standards were developed to be helpful in everyday life, but they prove indispensable when dealing with the ambiguities associated with international travel. The nine standards and the questions associated with them, as found in Figure 6.3, set the stage for better thinking when engaged in travel (Paul & Elder, 2009). While I make

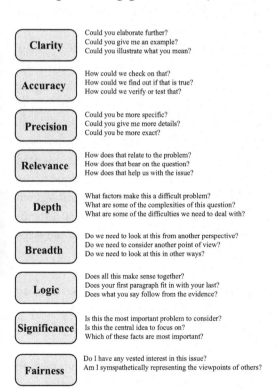

**Clarity**
Could you elaborate further?
Could you give me an example?
Could you illustrate what you mean?

**Accuracy**
How could we check on that?
How could we find out if that is true?
How could we verify or test that?

**Precision**
Could you be more specific?
Could you give me more details?
Could you be more exact?

**Relevance**
How does that relate to the problem?
How does that bear on the question?
How does that help us with the issue?

**Depth**
What factors make this a difficult problem?
What are some of the complexities of this question?
What are some of the difficulties we need to deal with?

**Breadth**
Do we need to look at this from another perspective?
Do we need to consider another point of view?
Do we need to look at this in other ways?

**Logic**
Does all this make sense together?
Does your first paragraph fit in with your last?
Does what you say follow from the evidence?

**Significance**
Is this the most important problem to consider?
Is this the central idea to focus on?
Which of these facts are most important?

**Fairness**
Do I have any vested interest in this issue?
Am I symspathetically representing the viewpoints of others?

**Figure 6.3** The Universal Intellectual Standards

each traveler aware of these standards, I use them myself in checking their statements about cultural learning. It would be too cumbersome and time-consuming to employ each specifically and directly to probe every statement a traveler makes in discussing the experience, but as rules of thumb, they can be quite helpful.

Some examples in employing each of the standards, when discussing cultural immersion experiences follow:

**Clarity**: Clarity is referred to as the "gateway" standard (Ibid.). When engaged with unfamiliar environments and cultures it's even more essential to take steps to ensure absolute clarity—in as far as that's possible. The best method in conversational settings is simple restatement, "I hear you saying . . ." or, "What I heard you say is . . ." or, "If I've heard you correctly, you're telling me . . . ." While it may slow the conversation a bit, the time commitment is well worth the investment. It may be best to always assume meaning must be confirmed. The greater the complexity of the situation at hand, the greater the need for deliberate techniques to clarify meaning. Albert Einstein was purported to have said, "If you can't explain it simply, you don't understand it well enough."

Before, during and after culturally immersive experiences I look for teach-back opportunities. These can best be defined as methods of communication confirmation. Often associated with the healthcare industry, teach-back enables doctors to gauge patient information needs and understanding as well as measure the effectiveness of communication provided. One classic technique I encourage travelers to use is named for the great American theoretical physicist, Richard Feynman. An original member of the Manhattan Project and one of the most highly decorated physicists in history, he is perhaps best known today for his teaching techniques that clarify even the most difficult material. The so-called Feynman Technique involves four simple steps (Hustle Escape, 2020):

- **Choose a concept and learn about it**. I have travelers select an important topic about the culture we'll be visiting. It can be about anything. Nothing is off the table, but it must be something the presenter feels passionate about discussing.
- **Pretend to teach it to a child**. I ask the "instructor" to imagine they're speaking to five-year-olds when delivering the session and to speak slowly with exaggerated attempts to ensure understanding.

- **Review gaps in understanding**. I require the speaker to present an outline with pre-planned probing questions to ensure the understanding of their listener. After they've finished teaching the subject, I ask them to go back and fill in the gaps that were unveiled in the discussion. They won't master the concept on the second presentation, but they will come far closer to mastery when they debrief their discoveries with the entire group in the final check-in on the last day of travel.
- **Refine, organize and tell powerful stories**. Stories make things memorable. Stories become ever "stickier" when they're surprising, humorous and compelling. Employing graphic images can aid clarity. The more multi-sensory those images, the more effective.

I find the Feynman Technique extremely helpful to guide travelers to make the most of their limited preparation time. Their preparation, in turn, benefits everyone. Throughout the travel experience they "own" the subject and are usually quite proud to share the way their thinking has evolved during the trip.

**Accuracy**: In its most basic form, being accurate is defined as being free from errors and distortions. During the preparation phase, I ask travelers to find an article or story about the place they will be traveling that they suspect is inaccurate. I then ask them to do an online fact check of the material. I then ask them to bring that article or story with them and revisit it with the facts they draw from observations of events while actually on travel. Did direct observation change the fact pattern? How could they rewrite the article to make it more accurate?

**Precision**: In most scientific analyses, accuracy is defined as how closely a measure reveals true value. Precision involves the degree to which the measure can be consistently repeated under similar conditions. In the framework of Universal Intellectual Standards, precision refers to a level of detail or specificity. This is where the Socratic questioning mentioned earlier comes into play. The ability of travelers to interrogate their own beliefs, as well as those of their fellow travelers, evolves over time, but only if travelers are aware of the need for more precise thinking.

**Relevance**: The Intellectual Standard of relevance comes into play in two ways. At the meta-level, it's all too easy for people to take in the travel experience for pure entertainment value. The leader must remind everyone of the real purpose behind the trip often. In dynamic travel experiences, staying focused on the original purpose of the visit can be difficult. For example, I usually add practical subjects such as trekking techniques, first aid, camping basics and so on. Travelers too often over-emphasize the importance of such practical matters. These topics only represent a means to an end—all learning outcomes are rooted in cross-cultural competence. Constantly checking in on conversations to ensure they remain relevant to this purpose is a requirement. Small talk isn't forbidden but it must be minimized.

At the micro-level, individual conversations must be checked for relevance as well. In any teaching environment, it can be extremely difficult to keep some students from straying far afield of the topic at hand. When the classroom is a foreign environment with a confusing culture, travelers need even more help staying true to task. A red herring is an intentionally misleading statement meant to draw the listener away from the real issue or answer. This phenomenon seems more prevalent in immersive cross-cultural travel for reasons I have not fully investigated.

**Depth**: Of all the intellectual standards, depth may be the most difficult to address when engaged in international travel. Thinking through multiple and changing variables requires discipline. The concept of depth challenges us to examine deeply held assumptions and blind spots about people and place (Schon, 1983). On a good day, we may even unravel fixed beliefs, for those beliefs can be clear, accurate, precise, and relevant yet remain dangerously superficial. Educators have long sought to encourage deep thinking through reflective practice. Researchers such as John Dewey, Kurt Lewin and Jean Piaget developed detailed theories to aid learners in reflecting on their actions and experiences in such a way as to engage a process of continuous learning (Dewey, 1998[1933]). Among the most effective ways to encourage reflective practice is the daily debrief. Closely examining key experiences can be facilitated using the following checklist:

- **Describe:** "What happened? Compare differing perceptions."
- **Feel:** "What were your reactions and feelings? How do they compare with others?"
- **Evaluate:** "What was good or bad about the experience?"

- **Analyze:** "What sense can you make of the situation? What was really going on? Were different people's experiences similar or different in important ways?"
- **Conclude: (general)** "What have you concluded, in a general sense, about your reaction to being immersed in a foreign culture?"
- **Conclude: (specific)** "What can you conclude about the specific culture in which you were immersed?"
- **Develop: (A Personal Action Plan):** "What are you going to do differently in this type of situation next time? Can you develop a framework that will make you more cross-culturally competent in the future?"

(adapted from Duke & Murphy, 2011)

Daily group debriefs can model sound reflective practice, but must be followed up with encouragement to do this individually. A journal is the best tool for individual reflection. I ask students to briefly share their journals with me at the conclusion of the travel.

**Breadth:** Thinking broadly requires we consider multiple perspectives and see situations and people from multiple vantage points. The world is an infinitely complex place. Cultures are multifactorial phenomena, yet we create stories and viewpoints that attempt to reduce culture to a single characterization. Being broad-minded, as opposed to narrow-minded, demands we reason generously. Taking in the point of view of others requires empathetic reasoning. We can define empathy as "the action of understanding, being aware of, being sensitive to, and vicariously experiencing the feelings, thoughts, and experience of another of either the past or present without having the feelings, thoughts, and experience fully communicated in an objectively explicit manner" (Merriam-Webster, n.d.). We can practice empathy by building language habits. Examples of everyday language that encourages empathy include:

- This sounds like a tough situation for you . . .
- I can only imagine how you must feel about . . .
- You sound very angry about . . . how can I help?
- I see how this is so important to you . . . .

Sometimes you can never fully know someone else's perspective unless you ask for it. Finding the words to do so can be a tremendous aid to communication and understanding.

**Logic**: Reasoning conducted or assessed according to strict principles of validity is the most direct path to effective problem-solving. The human brain tries to make order and sense out of the world. When immersed in foreign cultures it's always helpful to follow the evidence anytime someone makes a statement of fact or provides a story to explain a situation, person or thing. There are many theoretical constructs and working definitions of logic. For the purpose of cross-cultural competence development, it's helpful to narrow the working definitions to argumentation theory, or more simply "argumentation."

An argument's structure is comprised of a set of assumptions or premises, a method of reasoning or deduction, and a concluding point. We use argument to persuade, negotiate, inquire, deliberate and inform. Culture has an incredibly strong influence on all of these factors. Therefore, it can be extremely helpful to develop an "argument map" in order to see its component parts. An example is found in Figure 6.4.

**Significance**: To be significant is to be worthy of attention. As we make meaning of our environment and experiences we naturally prioritize or rank-order concepts. I like to begin discussions in this regard

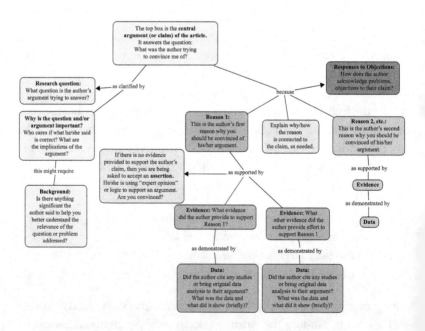

**Figure 6.4** Argument map template

by starting with values—ours, theirs and how they differ. Values are statements of the worth or the usefulness of something. Values have intrinsic worth but vary among cultures and individuals. This is the primary reason why good and reasonable people can disagree. Some of our cherished values are individually driven and are thought to be innate while others are purely the product of our culture. Cultural clashes tend to be rooted in value differences. That's why the questions such as, "What seems to be of greatest value to the people here?" and, "How does that differ from your own value judgments?" and, "How are they similar?" are so important to explore.

**Fairness**: Lastly, fairness is freedom from bias, deception and selfish-interest. There is no more foundational aspect to cross-cultural competence than a mindset of determined fairness. This can be expressed in a variety of ways:

- **Interactional Justice**: appropriateness of how we treat each other.
- **Procedural Justice**: appropriateness of rules used to allocate goods, benefits or other outcomes.
- **Distributive Justice**: appropriateness in how we actually distribute those goods, benefits and outcomes.
- **Social Justice**: equality and solidarity in a culture or society.

During debriefs I encourage travelers to interrogate vested interests—their own as well as those of others. Do those interests result in unfairness or injustice to anyone? Since I've spent so many years of my life teaching ethics, these conversations tend toward the philosophical (e.g. what are our duties to others? How do we weigh the net happiness created by our actions without privileging our selfish interests over others? etc.).

### OTHER HELPFUL HEURISTICS TO AID CRITICAL THINKING

Heuristics are simple rules of thumb that help us come to better conclusions. They inform us enough to, at minimum, make an educated guess. Long before people used the term heuristic, philosophers used the term "razor." The notion of a "razor" to shave off unlikely explanations for a phenomenon is centuries old. Perhaps the original example of such a device is Occam's razor, so named for the Franciscan Friar William of Ockham (also Occam) c. 1287–1347, although the principle attributed to him wasn't coined until centuries after his death (Sober, 2015). Sometimes referred to as the principle of parsimony, Occam's razor asks us, when presented with an array of options, to simply choose the one with the fewest assumptions. In dynamic environments encountered on international travel, knowing simple rules of thumb can be extremely helpful when navigating unfamiliar terrain and cultures. I have used Occam's Razor many times with travelers when we've encountered seemingly unexplainable phenomena by nudging them with the question: "All things being equal, simpler explanations are generally better than complex ones . . . so how do we best make sense of what we're experiencing?"

While I've used Occam's razor most frequently, I've also encouraged travelers to consider other well-known heuristics as shown in Table 6.5 (Life Lessons, n.d.).

While none of these heuristics or razors is infallible, they are a reasonably good place to start when trying to take in immensely complex and novel cultural dynamics. In their own way, each requires that we

**Table 6.5** Well-known heuristics

| | |
|---|---|
| **Hanlon's razor** | Never attribute to malice that which is adequately explained by incompetence or stupidity. People usually don't mean to harm you or have bad intentions, they just don't know any better. |
| **KISS principle** | Let's not make this too hard on ourselves (Keep It Simple Stupid). |
| **Hume's razor** | Causes must be sufficiently able to produce the effect assigned to them. |
| **Popper's principle** | For a theory to be considered scientific, it must be possible to disprove or refute it. |
| **Alder's razor** | If something cannot be settled by experiment, it is not worth debating. |
| **Duck test** | If it looks like a duck, swims like a duck, and quacks like a duck, then it probably is a duck. |
| **Grice's razor** | Address what the speaker actually meant, instead of addressing the literal meaning of what they actually said. (This can be quite difficult.) |
| **Hitchens razor** | What can be asserted without evidence can be dismissed without evidence. |
| **Sagan standard** | Extraordinary claims require extraordinary evidence. |

give our hosts, and ourselves, grace. Human nature is to overreact and draw negative, hasty conclusions. This is as unfair as it is unnecessary. A few good rules of thumb are often all we need on the path to being cross-culturally competent.

## CONCLUSION

Critical thinking is difficult. Thinking critically when navigating unfamiliar terrain, trying to communicate without knowing the local language, being slightly ill because you ate something strange, and so on can make critical thinking seem to be an entirely impossible undertaking. After engaging in travel to more than 60 countries, I have concluded, however, that it is not impossible. Being aware of biases generally, but in particular the biases that you and your fellow travelers are most susceptible to, is a good starting point. Writing about those biases in a journal and engaging in guided discussions about them should be continuous. Awareness of methods to limit biased thinking only improves your odds of a successful travel experience. Habituating yourself and your team in the best practices of critical thinking leads eventually to the elusive and essential skill of cross-cultural competence. Make liberal use of checklists and rules of thumb on that journey. Your reward will be great.

## REFERENCES

DellOrgfano, R. (2020). The great equalizer: True learning requires neither gold nor pedigree, in *New Oxford Review*, November.

Dewey, J. (1998[1938]). *How we think: A restatement of the relation of reflective thinking to the educative process*. Boston, MA: Houghton Mifflin.

Dodge, N. (2007). *The brain that changes itself: Stories of personal triumph from the frontiers of brain science*. New York, NY: Penguin.

Duke, W., & Murphy, J. (2011). *The debrief imperative*. New York, NY: FastPencil.

Foundation for Critical Thinking (n.d.). Retrieved from www.criticalthinking.org/

Hustle Escape (blog) (2020). The Feynman technique: 4 steps to learn anything. Retrieved from www.hustleescape.com

Kahneman, D., Sibony, O., & Sunstein, R. (2021). *Noise: A flaw in human judgment*. New York, NY: Little, Brown Spark.

Life Lessons (n.d.). 9 Philosophical Razors You Need to Know. Retrieved from www.lifelessons.co

*Merriam-Webster Dictionary* (n.d.) Definition of "empathy." Retrieved from www.merriam-webster.com/dictionary/empathy

Park, D., & Huang, C-M. (2010). Culture wires the brain: A cognitive neuroscience perspective. *Perspectives on Psychological Science*, 5(4), 391–400.

Paul, R., & Elder, L. (2009). *Critical thinking: Concepts & tools*. Tomales, CA: Foundation for Critical Thinking.

Schon, D. (1983). *The reflective practitioner: How professionals think in action*. New York, NY: Basic Books.

Schwartz, T. (2018). What it takes to think deeply about complex problems. *Harvard Business Review*, May.

Sober, E. (2015). *Ockham's razor: A user's manual*. London: Cambridge University Press.

Taylor, A. E. (1989). *Socrates*. Norwalk, CT: Easton Press.

# Seven

*Empathy, Mindfulness and Reflexivity*

CLEMENTINE K. FUJIMURA

## INTRODUCTION

From bolstering personal growth to optimizing outcomes in unfamiliar contexts, cross-cultural competence (3C) offers a path to personal and professional fulfillment. However, as this book has pointed out, such fulfillment cannot be achieved simply by reading a manual. From the experiential component involving participant-observation to reflexivity (a dynamic awareness of one's relationship to people in different cultural contexts), 3C is developed and maintained through interaction, rumination, self-critique with resulting reflection, and insight into the behavior and motivations of others and oneself. In this chapter, we will focus on three key ingredients that pave the way to 3C and its optimization to make the process as seamless as possible. The key elements to be understood, discovered, fine-tuned and optimized are: empathy, mindfulness and reflexivity.

In developing 3C, much can be gleaned from the field of communication, in particular, the study of intercultural communication. As a reminder, 3C results in an ability to engage with new cultures, no matter one's familiarity with them. It is a skill and aptitude that challenges one's ability to adapt in unfamiliar surroundings. Intercultural communication is the outcome of cultures interacting with one another. It is the communicative process in which people of different cultural backgrounds communicate. Ting-Toomey (1993) points out that in intercultural communication, people become effective through repeated practice in routine interactions. In the traditional study of intercultural communication, it is often assumed that students must have a knowledge of the cultures involved. In 3C, as defined in this book, knowledge of the cultures involved is a "nice-to-have" component, but not necessary.

The field of intercultural communication identifies the subtle underlying cognitive components that are imperative for 3C.

DOI: 10.4324/9781003213352-8

Matsumoto (2011) emphasizes the role of emotions in communicative acts and posits that emotion must be regulated in order for an intercultural interaction to be effective. During the communicative process, people desire being understood, respected and supported (Brabant et al., 2011: 29). Both parties in intercultural communication will achieve mutually optimal outcomes if they are thoughtful rather than reactive—that is, if they practice empathy, mindfulness, and reflexivity.

In this chapter, we will distinguish between sympathy and empathy and elaborate on the role of empathy, mindfulness and reflexivity in developing 3C. Ensuing real-life situations explore the meaning of the interpersonal gap and how empathy can aid perspective-taking when a person is confronted with variations in cultural understandings and approaches to such concepts as what it takes to be "in" time and space. It is only when we can imagine ourselves as the "other," when we understand that basic ideas of being a group or family member are culturally unique and tied up in concepts such as time and space, that we can shift our points of view and engage in meaningful, respectful and supportive ways with people from different backgrounds.

### DISCOVERING EMPATHY

Empathy falls into the category of both a skill and an aptitude that is learned. It is not to be confused with sympathy, though we often use empathy and sympathy synonymously. Milton J. Bennett, a sociologist who created the Developmental Model for Intercultural Sensitivity (1993), distinguishes between the two by pointing out that sympathy is similarity based, stemming from a monocultural mindset, whereas empathy is difference-based, stemming from an intercultural mindset.

Sympathy is the result of placing oneself in another person's position, that is, pondering how you would feel if you were in that person's situation. Sympathy can result in the action of treating others as one would like to be treated. The assumption of sympathy is that all humans are more similar than different and thus would want to be treated as you do: "Sympathy as projection . . . we merely assume that the other person is like ourselves and therefore impute to him or her our own thoughts and feelings" (Bennett, 1998: 197). Studies have shown, however, that cultural differences—including ethnic, socio-economic, professional, educational, religious, and the like—underlie different expectations of treatment. Sympathy is insensitive to difference, can be patronizing and can breed defensiveness in an interaction (Ibid.: 202).

Empathy, on the other hand, is the result of you imagining how other people feel given their unique perspectives that are unlike our own, "the imaginative intellectual and emotional participation in another person's experience" (Ibid.: 207). Empathy relies on one's ability to participate in another person's activity and to practice perspective-taking (Ibid.). The assumption of empathy is that all humans are different. For empathy to be effective, one must engage in self-reflection and conceive of oneself as the "other": "If we accept that we might be different, be given different constructions and circumstances, then we are free to imagine our thoughts and feelings from that different perspective" (Ibid.: 209). Empathy can be developed through immersive experiences and journaling with the goal of: "Do unto others as they themselves would have done unto them" (Ibid.: 213).

Let us take, for example, traditions and rituals. Traditions are practices that are passed on from one generation to the next. Rituals are culturally prescribed symbolic procedures that guide members through transitions and also reinforce a sense of community. Cultures vary in both performance and types of traditions and rituals. While we may be able to sympathize with certain individual human circumstance, say in the case of death, we may not necessarily understand the significance of rituals surrounding that circumstance in a foreign cultural context. We understand our own but not necessarily others' reactions to situations. While we can sympathize with the fact that death is sad, it is harder to empathize; that is, to understand the event in terms of another person's unique cultural history—the social impact and the significance of the ritual as an expression of community or as a means to ensure social continuity in a given region. For example, the act of lamenting or mourning holds varying significance depending on the society: Whereas in one society a lament can be an individual expression of grief, in another society it is performed as a ritual that communicates not only personal grieving, but possibly regional distinction, varying relations to the deceased or social hierarchy. Thus, if a ritual is incorrectly enacted, that is, when a person mourns inappropriately, it can be seen as a sign of disrespect.

Rituals surrounding death vary globally and it is important for cross-cultural relationship building to understand variations and empathizing with culturally unique expressions of grief. Linguist Helga Kotthoff (2006) has analyzed the grieving process of Magrelian (an ethnic subgroup of Georgia found in northwestern Georgia and parts of Abkhasia and Tblisi) and East Georgian cultures. She has found that, while across these regions similar lamentations in the event of a death can be found, the differences in performance and the extent to which outsiders and insiders are attuned to these differences determines the success of the ritual—the way in which people think about and respect each other. Inappropriate lamentation may create intercultural conflict. In general, anthropologists have found that seemingly instinctive behaviors such as laughter or crying cannot be interpreted from an outsider's personal standpoint but rather, we need more insider information to laugh and cry appropriately. This information includes correct timing of behavior adjusted to specific contexts and knowledge of the relationship among verbal, para- and non-verbal aspects (Kotthoff, 2006: 295).

> The forms of mourning index regional identities . . . Thus, in lamentation, women from Margrelia and Guria scratch their faces [this gesture is found in many cultures]; in East Georgia, these forms are regarded as exaggerated . . . and artificial [ar namdvili]. In West Georgia, fainting is an expression of a woman's extreme grief. In East Georgia, it is strongly rejected.
>
> (Ibid.: 297)

If a person is an outsider, he or she may appropriately abstain from lamenting either because it is not customary or because the outsider's style might be perceived as offensive. Culturally appropriate styles of lamentation can engender the expected emotional response from members of the community. For an East Georgian engaged in mourning, customary West Georgian laments are ineffective. One such reaction is the West Georgian "tirili" (crying), a behavior that affects, underscores and engenders sadness in the community. This practice does not make a person in East Georgia sad (Ibid.: 199). Within a region, appropriate wailing, lamenting or crying reinforces the emotion, but it does not do the same in another region. An important criterion of a lament within a region is its ability to encourage and move others to genuinely cry. Not only does appropriate lamenting and wailing affect insiders, it helps distinguish who are the outsiders, the "we" and the "you," while reinforcing feelings (Ibid.: 300–301). Knowing the nuances of such a death ritual is just one example of many other rituals that enhance our understanding of cultures and illustrate the significance of expressions and behaviors. The ability to understand the other's point of view, to have empathy, allows us to predict behaviors, negotiate cultural contexts and to adapt to, and coordinate, interactions competently.

Without empathy, interactions can be fraught with beliefs that are detrimental to cross-cultural competence and thus to a successful outcome. Roy J. Eidelson and Judy I. Eidelson (2003) elaborate on five belief domains that can yield conflict between groups. These include the belief in one's superiority; that injustice is being done; feelings of vulnerability; distrust; and helplessness at the individual and group levels.

Shared convictions of moral superiority represent ethnocentric monoculturalism, a mindset detrimental to compromise and expressions of forgiveness and apology. The belief in injustice or a sense of victimization is analyzed as a powerful if not main motivation for war. Vulnerability adds to the list of belief domains by magnifying the power of fear when a person or community does not feel safe; as with the other domains, vulnerability can lead to hostility, ethnocentrism and territorialism. Distrust and helplessness feed these negative outcomes as well, further sapping communities of resilience and contributing to a mindset of powerlessness (Eidelson & Eidelson, 2003).

These negative outcomes can be due to an individual's lacking in the fundamental and initial process of empathy. By taking the time to develop empathy, conflict can be mitigated. Empathy allows people to build trust, create a sense of safety, communicate respectfully and collaborate. While it is not necessary for people to abandon their own perspective, the ability to empathize, to feel and think as if they were in the other person's or group's place, allows for individual perspectives to expand and to include the other's viewpoint. It is a dialogic process, one in which individuals interact across cultural boundaries, listen respectfully, continually reflect, and are curious about and open to new information. Via the development of empathy, seemingly contrasting worldviews can come together such that a new worldview is created and via which people can work together, negotiate and coexist (see Broome, 2015: 288–289).

## MINDFULNESS AND REFLEXIVITY

3C involves an interplay of fundamental abilities. For one, as discussed above, there is the need for empathy. Equally foundational, however, is the practice of mindfulness: the ability to interact with people from different cultural backgrounds while maintaining one's awareness of one's own cultural values and expected behaviors (see Brabant et al., 2007: 55–75). However, for mindfulness to aid in 3C, it must be combined with reflexivity: the practice (and art) of scrutinizing one's own beliefs, values and judgments in a given social context and considering how these might influence ensuing interactions in that context.

The practice of mindfulness is often relegated to the spiritual domain and yet it can be quite practical: It is reflective/reflexive, effectively guiding intentional interactions. Mindfulness involves reflexivity to consider one's own and others' assumptions, reactions, intentions, aptitudes and behaviors. Both mindfulness and reflexivity require that a person be fully present and non-judgmental.

The concept of reflexivity in the social sciences has come to mean thinking carefully about the individuals involved in an interaction: how or under what conditions an interaction takes place, by whom, and what impact personalities and context might have on the outcomes:

> Mindful reflexivity requires us to tune in to our own cultural and personal habitual assumptions in scanning a communication scene. It also means "emptying our mind-set" and de-cluttering the internal noises so that we can listen with an in-the-moment pure heart.
>
> (Ting-Toomey, 1993: 621)

The ability to enter an interaction with mindful reflexivity occurs developmentally, and developing this ability requires continuous attention.

Being aware of personal ethnocentric views is a first step in mindfulness for cross-cultural competence. Once we ascertain what judgments we hold, we can manage emotional energy and employ open-mindedness, cultural curiosity, and adaptability in unfamiliar contexts. Managing emotional energy is of utmost importance. When a situation is tense, it is easy not to listen to others and to be consumed by one's own emotions. Mindfulness thus requires that we practice non-judgment not only of others, but also of ourselves, including our own emotional state:

> Practicing unconditional acceptance of and watchfulness over one's own arising emotional state as part of the field of experience may help tone down the escalating internal stress. Externally, cultivating emotional attunement with the other person's affective states . . . may help create some constructive space.
>
> (Ibid.: 623)

Cultivating mindfulness—through observation, listening, attunement and reframing one's perspective—is helpful in regulating and being mindful of one's own reactions and perspectives and those of others. Attunement in particular demands cultural empathy and may benefit from meditation and breathing techniques.

Much has been written on training proper breathing for regulating emotions. According to medical researchers, even slight changes in one's breathing can enhance physical performance, aid in medical recovery, and control anxiety. Dating back thousands of years, ancient breathing practices were lauded for reinforcing patience, improving physical and emotional flexibility, and creating an awareness of our surroundings. Breathing techniques are one means to control our moods and emotions:

> [Breathing techniques] give us the means to stretch our lungs and straighten our bodies, boost blood flow, balance our minds and moods, and excite the electrons in our molecules . . . They offer a mystery and magic of life that unfolds a little more with every new breath we take.
>
> (Nestor, 2020: 202).

Proper breathing can control heart rate, help concentration and mindfulness and reduce stress. In unfamiliar or uncomfortable human interactions, proper breathing can help defuse stress. Combining the ingredients of an open aptitude, mindfulness, reflexivity, empathy and respect will lay the foundation for cross-cultural competence.

## THE EXPERIENCE OF EMPATHY AND MINDFULNESS: THE INTERPERSONAL GAP

What motivates one person does not necessarily motivate another, and responding appropriately requires work. In 1967, John L. Wallen, a social psychologist, wrote an unpublished paper entitled "The Interpersonal Gap." The Interpersonal Gap refers to that space of uncertainty and unintended consequences in communication. It is a rift that occurs when the outcome of a conversation was not as expected. As Wallen points out, often in interpersonal dialogue, "what you accomplish is not always what you hoped" (Wallen, 1967: 1).

This was precisely what happened with a woman we'll call "Connie," who led a wilderness survival expedition involving a small group of people. Because Connie came to the expedition with no canyoneering skills and was nervous, she explained her fears to the group right from the start. Like many individuals, she thought that by sharing her worries, she was not only establishing her strengths and weaknesses, but also building relationships: She was certain that others shared her concerns and assumed they would feel good that she, their chosen leader, could identify with them. Research on gender communication points to this tendency of wanting to bond as a primary motivator for communication among women in the United States:

> For most women, the language of conversations is primarily
> a language of rapport: a way of establishing connections and
> negotiating relationships. Emphasis is placed on displaying
> similarities and matching experiences.
>
> (Tannen, 1990: 77)

Especially in unfamiliar or precarious contexts, human proclivities become more pronounced, causing us to sink into our personal comfort zone, latching on to what feels right. Diligently, albeit possibly frantically, Connie reported at every turn what she noticed, and what she was thinking and feeling, hoping subconsciously for affirmation from team members that they were thinking and feeling the same.

What she neglected to consider is that others might not react to the environment and stress the same way she did.

The group Connie led that day was made up of three men. People who identify as male, according to research in sociolinguistics, tend to build rapport not by expressing distress or angst, but rather through shared activities (Ibid.: 85). Rather than find comfort in her emotional honesty, the men were turned off. While they too shared her concerns, Connie's style of rapport building was more detrimental than effective. According to Waller's theory, she had created an interpersonal gap: The intent of the communication was not received. For her to have been successful in this group of male professionals, in order to create a feeling of team spirit on a physically challenging expedition, she needed to let her personal inclinations go and be in the present, practice empathy and adjust to the group: to be "in." Being "in" requires observing, listening, being present, discovering the other perspectives, being reflexive and adapting. In other words: practicing cross-cultural competence.

### RELATIONSHIPS AND WHAT IT TAKES TO BE "IN"

To be "in" requires constant evaluation of one's effects on the surrounding human terrain. Let's take for example a trip by an exchange student we'll call "Will." Will is biracial, has roots in Germany and had visited Germany with his family prior to the exchange. With his travels came knowledge and experience of being an "in" person and an "out" person. Subconscious biases in many German villages include notions of who is part of the village and who is not. For example, in some Bavarian towns, tourism is seen as both an asset and a threat. As Mr. Salzer, a farmer in the Chiemsee region of Bavaria explained:

> We were a poor region of Germany until tourists started coming here on vacation. Our farmers could barely hold their own but now, because of tourism, my farm has become a getaway and I can support it largely due to vacationers (mostly from other German areas), some of whom are regulars. Nice people and all, but they do change our peaceful way of life and that irks me sometimes. We have more traffic, pollution, and they even belittle us and make fun of some of our traditions. It's like we are in a zoo. Plus, younger generations are

starting to doubt our culture because of outsiders. They don't get it so
I am wary of them.

(Mr. Salzer, 2018, personal communication)

Will knew that by appearing in a Bavarian village, he would stand out as one of the tourists, very possibly as a foreigner, and that Bavarians might be less interested in getting to know him and welcome him. Right at the outset of his visit at an outdoor Biergarten, Will noticed people being curt with him at the rather long table. (In a Biergarten, people share tables and may socialize with each other beyond their peer group.) It was not until Will shared information about his family, "themselves Bavarians and thus myself as having familial and cultural ties to Bavaria," he says, "that people truly opened up and we had a fabulous evening. Indeed, by telling people of my family in Bavaria, I was able to make friends certainly more quickly and lasting." By knowing the deep-seated sentiments surrounding who is "in" and who is "out," Will was able to take advantage of his "in-ness" and be trusted. He empathized with their point of view and was mindful in his interactions, appropriately careful to get to know the people at the table step by step, respectful of them and ultimately proving that he was to be trusted. Not everyone can claim such an advantage when traveling, but knowing the way in which people view an outsider is a good step in figuring out ways to break down barriers.

Ironically, similar to our experience of people not being open to Americans as we travel outside the United States, people from across the globe visiting the U.S. may consider northern Americans living in northern regions to be closed off to them. At times, this is due to differences in cultural understandings of key concepts such as friendship, family, age groups, time and space. A visitor from Kenya notes:

Americans appear to us rather distant. They are not really as close
to other people—even fellow Americans—as Americans overseas
tend to portray. It's like building a wall. Unless you ask an American a
question, he will not even look at you. Individualism is very high.

(Kohls & Knight, 1994: 44)

Another similar impression is that Americans are not sincere when they say they would like to get to know another person. A common observation from international visitors: "So often I meet someone in the United States and we part with the promise that 'we must get together sometime' and then they never call!" Some visitors will take on the challenge and very quickly call that person only to be surprised that the person does not have time, or that that in turn might mean they did not actually intend to get together. A visitor from Indonesia notes: "Americans look warm, but when a relationship starts to become personal, they try to avoid it," and, "It is puzzling when Americans apply the word 'friend' to acquaintances from almost every sector of one's past or present life, without necessarily implying close ties or inseparable bonds" (Ibid.). Indeed, the connotation of friend is, in practice, not universal.

When it comes to relationships, the notions of friend, kin and family (nuclear or extended) are complicated and not to be assumed as the same as one's own. How often have you heard someone refer to someone as "so-and-so is a friend of mine?" In the United States people call someone a friend when they connect on a certain level and spend time together. As time goes by, however, they may or may not stay in touch and some friendships will be deeper than others. A relationship that is more casual may not preclude an American from calling a person a friend. To people from countries such as Germany or Russia, such casual friends might better be described as acquaintances. Americans may use these terms interchangeably. Consider this insight shared by an exchange student from the United States:

When I first came to Russia in 2005, people seemed very cold and withdrawn from me. It was hard to get to know people, much less be invited to their homes. Living in a small town, which I assumed would be friendly, was instead a lonely experience. Finally, with time, I believe I can honestly say I made a few friends. But only a few. The problem I encountered was, however, a feeling of guilt. Once I was invited, it appeared the family members of my "friend" were overwhelmingly good to me. I mean, they offered me the best of what they had to eat and drink, even though it was obviously not easy for them to acquire such things like caviar, good meat, fancy champagne, and the like. How could I ever repay them? How could I ever return their friendship? Of course, I never came to their home without a gift, but somehow they would always outdo me with their hospitality.

(Matthew, 2020, personal communication)

Many a traveler to Russia has had this experience: In Russia, a friend is an important relationship, one that is cherished and not taken lightly. Words to distinguish between categories of acquaintances and friendship are not used interchangeably but rather carefully because the expectations and responsibilities in these relations are uniquely distinct. The list includes degrees of closeness: *znakomyi* (acquaintance), *priyatel'* (closer acquaintance) and *drug* (close friend). Sometimes even kinship terms are used to underscore the closeness of a friend. While similar terms exist in the English language, Americans are less careful to distinguish between them in casual conversation. Knowing the nuances of relationship terminology will be helpful in navigating personal and professional interactions abroad.

Beyond friendship, who is kin, who is not and the overall value placed on various kinship relations varies cross-culturally, as well. Kinship is not simply about who is related to whom, but also the mutual expectations, responsibilities of members and the membership of nuclear and extended families. A family may include simply a parent and a child, or a family may include grandparents or even the family pet. Not all families include children. In the United States and in many parts of the world in the 21st century families are complex and are being created and recreated in sundry ways, with LGBTQ+ parents and adoptions, for example. Within the complexity, however, are the ties that matter the most—those of family, through which people become who they are and establish a sense of connection, identity and well-being.

For some developing societies, family can be both emotionally and pragmatically binding. The value placed on extended family ties is traditionally strong in Japan, for example, although changes are occurring there as well. At first glance, the Japanese nuclear family appears much like that in the United States, leading to a presumption that the value of the family is the same in both societies. However, Japanese culture places a high value on loyalty to the inner group by birth and is thus less individualistic. Because of the focus on the collective and in particular, the family, it is likely even today to find a grandparent or two as part of the nuclear family in Japan and to find respect given to elders in general.

The importance of having a large family, of being a part of something greater than the self, places a burden on modern urbanizing

Optimizing 3C with Empathy, Mindfulness and Reflexivity

families. To tackle this issue in Japan, one company offers "rent-a-family." Grandparents may rent grandchildren and vice versa to make up for the loss of relatives.

> Weddings are the bread and butter of the rental-relative business, perhaps because traditions that dictate the number of guests haven't changed to reflect increasing urbanization and migration, shrinking families, and decreased job security.
>
> (Batuman, 2018)

Substituting the family members with pretend family members can create the appearance of an ideal family and demonstrates the value of strong family ties, even as society changes and people find it harder to maintain traditional expectations.

Being able to distinguish collectivist values is imperative when attempting to forge good working relations. Prior to becoming an English teacher in Japan, Dr. Erica Zimmerman, now a scholar and professor of Japanese language and culture, spent the early years of her immersion in Japan teaching English in a remote part of the country. To go anywhere other than her classes, she needed to use public transportation or a personal vehicle. While Dr. Zimmerman did have access to a train, it was a $12 round-trip and cumbersome. Ideally, she would have liked to have her own personal vehicle:

> When I lived in Japan, the Board of Education including the Head of the school I was assigned to accepted me and was in charge of me. I noticed that all the other teachers had cars and so one of the families I knew helped me to look for one. As is standard in Japan, I needed to let the Head of the school know and ask for permission. After all, she was officially responsible for me and were something to go wrong, she and the entire school could lose face and with that, their good reputation. Still, I persisted feeling that I would be fine and asking why I couldn't have one. Consistently the response was: "It's a bad idea." Finally, one day, it appeared my wish had been granted: I was given permission under the condition that I attend a one day driving class. This was not a big deal for me so I agreed, not knowing at the time that this had been my way out of a bad situation: I had pushed the Head and I should not have. I could simply walk away from

the request and go back to taking the train. Instead, I took the class and got my car. However, from that day on, things were never the same: I was no longer accepted as a part of the community, no longer invited to functions. I had lost face and was given the cold shoulder from the entire Board of Education, the collective, because I had been individualistic and only thought of my own needs.

(Zimmerman, 2020, personal communication)

In a society that values the collective, it is imperative that members and visitors are aware of the repercussions that behaviors can have on a larger community and to respect the community input beyond personal desires. Rules and expectations are oftentimes misunderstood by outsiders, and justifications can be difficult to define as they may have far greater cultural and even historical foundations and functions. Dr. Zimmerman now uses her experience to educate future officers as they prepare to live and work in Japan.

It is easy to fall into the trap of not considering the perspectives of others, often subconsciously maintaining that one's own perspective is the only one, and that peers and colleagues would agree. Especially in foreign contexts, when anxiety or culture shock can negatively impact daily interactions, it is easy to confuse sympathy with empathy. Being mindful of the possibility that our perspective at this given moment is out of place, not "in," allows for readjustment, and taking time to breathe, reflect and re-center.

## A FOCUS TIME AND SPACE

When entering a new community, honing in on the unique organization of time and space is invaluable. The way in which people perceive and value time and space, organize them, and react to them are significant tools in interactions and negotiations, the mutual understanding of which is imperative for positive outcomes.

How do people organize their day? How do they relate to the concept of time, if at all? Is time something to be managed because of certain beliefs or values, or is time perceived as taking a back seat to other things such as a possibly lengthy process of building relations? How do people build professional relationships? How is a professional space organized? How do people of a given social group organize their space? How do they organize their personal space? Is it different from yours? A community that values taking time to build relations—whether it be over a meal or through many meetings—rather than jumping to make decisions prior to establishing the relationship is not a community that does not value time. It is the degree to which one thing takes precedence over another that is important.

The idea that different cultures may understand time variously was explored by anthropologist E. T. Hall in 1959 (Hall, 1976). He labeled the contrasting conceptualizations as monochronic/sequential, as in the United States and many northern European countries, and polychronic/synchronic, as he saw in countries of, for example, South America. In the former he saw time as being associated with the importance of schedules and punctuality, whereas the latter focused more on people:

> This preoccupation with people is not socializing in the true sense, but more a recognition that in these cultures people are important (some more than others—family and superiors at work) and should be involved and attended to, even at the cost of interruption or distraction.
>
> (Adams & van Eerde, 2010: 765)

People traveling on business to polychronic cultures (especially in warmer climates) as in Brazil, Mexico, Spain and Indonesia often comment on issues of scheduling. Changes in meeting times and delays of deadlines are common. Scholars point to cultural differences in priorities, where the delay may be less a matter of not valuing time, but rather of prioritizing the present in front of future orientation, valuing "going with the flow," and being more flexible:

> The Spanish frequently employ the words "flexibilidad" and "inflexibilidad," the former as a virtue and the latter often as a failing, especially with regard to punctuality, rather than precise or imprecise. Modern Spaniards would usually allow five to ten minutes leeway depending on the importance of the event or the person (people) involved. Very few meetings or events actually start on time or with everyone present, but lateness or unpunctuality of this nature is not really classified as such. A different interpretation of the meaning of time use could also have affected responses.
>
> (Ibid.: 772)

A study on use of time indicates that in Spain the focus is on relationship-building as opposed to punctuality. It is more important to spend time with people than to rush through meetings in the name of being punctual (Ibid.: 773).

Cultural concepts such as time, family and friendship do not carry the same connotations in every culture. The exact connotations of these concepts and their components can significantly vary from culture to culture.

Like time, other seemingly obvious concepts such as space (personal or public) seem like they should be understood the same globally, but this is not the case. Consider this case of an American working and studying in Russia:

It was late and I was catching the last metro home in St. Petersburg. I usually loved taking the last metro because at this time of day, the cars are rather empty. During the day, the cars are sometimes so crowded that you have to wait for trains to come and go before you get squeezed in. I once lifted my leg off the floor and stayed in the air because I was being held up by the surrounding bodies! It gets very crowded. But on this night, the car was completely empty and I cherished the ability not only to find a seat, but to stretch out. At the next stop (I had at least five to go), a lady got on with a few bags. Would you believe it, she chose to sit right next to me. Not only next to me: her body was touching mine! I was surprised to say the least and wondered how I could move without offending her. I mean, I didn't know her or anything, but I just wanted space. Just for once! So, you know what I did? At the next stop, I got off and moved to another car . . . which was empty.

(Tina, 2018, personal communication)

As in many other countries, in Russia, personal space is perceived differently and the draw is to be close rather than distanced. When in a conversation in Russia, as well as in many other countries in the world, people tend to stand closer than is expected in the United States and it is common to see female friends or mother–daughter pairs walk with their arms intertwined. Stepping away from someone speaking to you can therefore be perceived as alienating. Sensitive to these cultural differences regarding personal space, Tina figured out a creative solution to preserve her own personal space and to avoid offending the woman on the train. Observing and thinking about personal space when travelling is another must.

## CONCLUDING REMARKS

With cultural empathy, adaptability, reflexivity and mindfulness as key elements, as outlined in this chapter, a next step might be to have a plan to achieving these developmental stages of 3C. Let us take a moment to organize states and stages to developing 3C aptitude:

- Be committed to learning about another's perspective
- Be in the moment
- Take time to reflect on the moment
- Ask for clarification to deepen understanding
- Take time to reflect and breathe both during the interaction and after (by journaling, for example)
- Take note of emotions felt or encountered
- Try to take the perspective of the other emotionally: their pain, their glee, or other
- Respond respectfully and with sensitivity "knowing that sometimes the power of silence may mean more than words."

(Adapted significantly from Ting-Toomey, 1993: 625).

Thinking about the meaning and goals of the other person's verbal and non-verbal cues will further perspective-taking and cultural empathy. Ultimately, 3C relies on adaptability, empathy and mindfulness, with the understanding that cross-cultural competence is never finished. It is a journey with many stops along the way.

## THOUGHT QUESTIONS

1. Seat yourself in a busy place (for example, an outdoor café or a mall). Close your eyes and take in the sounds. What sounds do you recognize? Which ones are unfamiliar? Open your eyes and find the source of the sounds.
2. Now open your eyes and look around you. What do you see that interests you? That repels you? What can you be curious about? How could you find out more?

3. Try to identify how your culture has shaped who you are?
4. Have you seen culture shaping another person or other people? How have people around you been socialized to behave?
5. What will be your first step today or tomorrow to try and see the world from a different perspective? Whose perspective will you try to take and how will you accomplish this?

## REFERENCES

Adams, S., & van Eerde, W. (2010). Time use in Spain: Is polychronicity a cultural phenomenon?. *Journal of Managerial Psychology*, 25, September, 764–776).

Batuman, E. (2018). Japan's rent-a-family industry. *The New Yorker*, April 23. Retrieved from www.newyorker.com/magazine/2018/04/30/japans-rent-a-family-industry, accessed November 17, 2020.

Bennett, M. J. (1993). Intercultural sensitivity. In *Principles of Training and Development* (pp. 185–206). Portland, OR: Portland State University.

Brabant, M., Watson, B., & Gallois, C. (2011). Psychological perspectives: Social psychology, language and intercultural communication. In D. Matsumoto (Ed.), *APA Handbook of Intercultural Communication* (pp. 23–39). Washington D.C.: American Psychological Association.

Brabant, M., Watson, B., & Gallois, C. (2007). Psychological perspectives: Social psychology, language, and intercultural communication. In H. Kotthoff & H. Spencer-Oatey (Eds.), *Handbook of Intercultural Communication*, vol. 7 (pp. 55–75). New York, NY: Mouton de Gruyer.

Broome, B. J. (2015). Empathy. In J. M. Bennet (Ed.), *The Sage Encyclopedia of Intercultural Competence*, Vol. 1 (pp. 286–289). Washington D.C.: Sage.

Eidelson, R. J., & Eidelson, J. I. (2003). Dangerous ideas: Five beliefs that propel groups toward conflict. *American Psychologist*, 58(3), 182–192.

Hall, E. T. (1976). *Beyond Culture*, New York, NY: Anchor Books.

Kohls, R. L., & Knight, J. M. (1994). *Developing intercultural awareness: A cross-cultural training handbook*, 2nd ed. Boston, MA: Intercultural Press.

Kotthoff, H. (2006). Communicating in intercultural lamentations in caucasian Georgia. In K. Buhrig & J. Thije (Eds.), *Beyond Misunderstanding* (pp. 289–311). Amsterdam: Benjamins.

Matsumoto, D. (2011). *APA handbook of intercultural communication*. Washington, D.C.: American Psychological Association, pp. 23–39.

Nestor, J. (2020). *Breath: The new science of a lost art*. New York, NY: Riverhead Books.

Tannen, D. (1990) *You just don't understand: Women and men in conversation*. New York, NY: Ballantine Books.

Ting-Toomey, S. (1993). Mindfulness. In J. M. Bennet (Ed.), *The Sage encyclopedia of intercultural competence* (pp. 620–626). Washington, D.C.: Sage.

Wallen, J. L. (1967). *Emotions as problems*. Portland, OR: Northwest Regional Educational Laboratory.

**INTERVIEWS**

Mr. Salzer, Summer 2018
Matthew, Fall 2020
Tina, 2018
Dr. Zimmerman, Summer 2020

Conclusion

# Eight

*The Personal and Organizational Benefits of Being Cross-Culturally Competent*

Joseph J. Thomas and Clementine K. Fujimura

In the first seven chapters of the book basic definitions, frameworks for understanding and systems for applying cross-cultural competence to leadership have been explored. In the end, this book is called a "Guide for Leaders" because it is designed to add value to people and organizations through this often-misunderstood capacity. On the personal level, elements of 3C are innate attributes—that is to say like personality, they are evolved from biological factors. Other elements are skill-based and can be learned. Mostly however, 3C at the personal level is attitudinal. Developing a mindset of 3C leads not only to more effective interaction when traveling, but to a state of enhanced well-being.

Similarly, individuals possessing 3C make organizations better—especially when those individuals are in positions of leadership. In turn, organizations or teams can make people better, especially if those teams are well led. During international travel, teams that deliberately incorporate the best practices of the *learning organization*, can create truly transformative experiences. 3C, at its best, is something that reframes everything about the way you see the world and your role in it. Armed with a handful of tools, leaders shape high-performing teams made up of high-functioning individuals.

## PERSONAL BENEFITS OF DEVELOPING 3C: EMPATHY AND COMPASSION

In the process of listening and learning about a diverse team at work, a leader increases a team's contentment. In a study conducted at MIT Sloan School of Management (see Sull & Sull, 2020), it was found that corporate culture ratings were surprisingly high during the COVID-19 pandemic. The spike in positive sentiment was directly related to a

DOI: 10.4324/9781003213352-9

sense that leaders communicated better: more transparently (disclosing actions and their basis), more fairly (just treatment without discrimination) and with integrity (honestly and ethically). Companies whose leadership was effective at communicating were perceived to harbor a concern for individual welfare and demonstrated agility in unprecedented contexts; in other words, they demonstrated 3C and had higher scores than those that did not demonstrate 3C.

Studies further point to the fact that communicating effectively and positively with others can lead to positive outcomes between people and, moreover, to a personal sense of well-being. Cultural adaptability has been associated with higher life satisfaction (Chen et al., 2019). When we develop the knowledge, skills and aptitudes for 3C, we not only increase work satisfaction, but we enrich ourselves personally. What we have offered in this book is an introduction to the skillset required for developing 3C for leaders as well as a skillset the readers who are team members can use to shape and sharpen personal growth. 3C beyond the workplace can be self-revelatory and deeply gratifying

Part of cultural adaptability challenges the individual to seek communication with others unlike themselves and to understand and accept cultural differences. In a study by Chen et al. (2019) Tibetan students who demonstrated strong ability to culturally adapt were found to possess better mental health with less anxiety and depression (Chen et al., 2019). Developing 3C allows for greater cultural adaptability in diverse settings and can lead to an increase in positive psychological outcomes such as optimism, which in turn stimulates a general sense of well-being.

In another study (Wesolowska et al., 2018), it was found that the skills for 3C, including cultural adaptability, acceptance, cultural curiosity, empathy and one's self-awareness, enable worker satisfaction. Nurses who were rated as having these skills had a higher sense of well-being and less incidence of psychological stress and fatigue. In particular, of all the knowledge, skills, abilities and aptitudes (KSAAs), the quality of empathy was most highly associated with well-being. It was concluded that empathy involves perspective taking which leads to effective intercultural communication and intercultural relationship building, all of which in turn promote psychological health.

Relating to others is a basic pro-social psychological human need for human socialization, which in turn produces endorphins, a process that decreases the sense of stress and elevates the pleasure effect (Pogosyan, 2018). 3C, because it involves perspective taking, empathy and compassion can contribute to the pleasure effect by increasing self-esteem and optimism (adapted from www.dartmouth.edu/wellness/emotional/rakhealthfacts.pdf). The process of developing cross-cultural competence can be personally fulfilling.

The personal benefit of 3C begins with being attuned to our own cultural selves, that is, our values and deep-rooted beliefs combined with a nonjudgmental openness to differences between people, that is to seek to understand and accept different views of the world. Through self-awareness and nonjudgment we can succeed at empathy. To recall from previous chapters in this book, empathy is "the use of imagination to intellectually and emotionally participate in an alien experience" and is not to be confused with sympathy in which we can know how we would experience a situation, but not how others might (Bennett, 1998: 221). According to Bennett (1998) empathetic responses to a new situation are successful in navigation and communicating across cultural boundaries whereas sympathetic responses are not. A person who simply believes that people are basically the same throughout the world was found to struggle with cross-cultural acceptance and adaptability. Essential to achieving adaptability is a constant effort on an individual's part to immerse themselves in new cultural contexts. The outcome of complex and varied cultural exposure helps us to tolerate differences more easily, and while it is challenging it is not threatening (Ibid.).

Ingredients that develop 3C have been valued throughout the ages in cultures and religions as important for our day-to-day lives and beyond. These ingredients have been known to societies as yielding personal and social peace. The Dalai Lama lists them among the "eight pillars of joy" or as he also calls them "qualities of the mind and heart" (Dalai Lama and Desmond Tutu, 2016: 282). Such qualities enable a state of balance and well-being. Of particular pertinence to 3C in the Dalai Lama's eight pillars are the qualities of perspective taking, acceptance and compassion (although each of the other pillars, humility, humor, forgiveness, gratitude and generosity can also be included as valuable to enabling effective leadership and communication).

In their conversation published in *The Book of Joy* (2016) the Dalai Lama and Archbishop Desmond Tutu agreed that, instead of focusing on the self, it behooves an individual to see the world from others' perspectives. In so doing, we "transcend our limited identity" and attain joy. This idea can be traced back to Buddhism which urges us to reduce our attachment to the notion of a personal identity. Instead, if we reduce our attachment to our identity, we break down barriers, can listen to others, and see the world through others' eyes. Via perspective taking we are able to empathize with others which, according to the Dalai Lama and the Archbishop, leads us to gain "humility, humor and acceptance" (Ibid.: 293–294).

Acceptance of others is born from empathy and is the gateway to moving forward in professional and personal relationships. If we understand others, we can accept them as who they are, whether or not we share in their experiences or responses to situations. Conflict arises from a reactive state, not from one of acceptance. In a reactive state, "we stay locked in judgment and criticism, anxiety and despair, even denial" (Ibid.: 329). Once we achieve acceptance we can respond more appropriately and effectively. Moreover, acceptance allows us to value, be grateful for and reap the benefits of differences. Through empathy and acceptance we can move on to compassion.

Compassion is a helpful quality in achieving personal fulfillment, but is distinguished from empathy. While empathy allows us to imagine and understand what a situation might be like for another person, it does not mean we share their feelings (sympathy) and it does not necessitate action. Compassion, however, elicits a response in which a person wants to help. The Dalai Lama explains the difference between empathy and compassion in an example: "if we see a person who is being crushed by a rock, the goal is not to get under the rock and feel what they are feeling; it is to help to remove the rock" (Ibid.: 380). In developing 3C, we might want to understand what a situation feels like, but if we take it a step further, we arrive at helping to ameliorate the situation for a person. This moment of compassion, when perspective taking has turned from a state of empathy to action, has been described as healing for the actor, even as elevating, as contributing to one's personal growth and feeling of well-being. Perhaps most importantly, 3C allows us to achieve new echelons of understanding and being as we form new relationships, try new customs and contemplate new values and behaviors. Through this development we experience deeply a continuous flow of growth, progress and becoming.

## ORGANIZATIONAL BENEFITS OF DEVELOPING 3C: ADAPTIVE CAPACITY AND THE LEARNING ORGANIZATION

Qualities such as compassion, empathy and acceptance are powerful elements for an individual seeking cross-cultural competence. When bound together in groups or teams, individuals possessing these qualities can create synergy that enables everyone to get more from an immersive experience. Generally speaking, people want more from interactions with unfamiliar cultures than acquiring language skills or mere exposure to novel situations. People want to reframe and expand their perspective. They want additional lenses through which to see, different approaches to problem solving, and new means by which to understand their own lives. All of this is best accomplished in groups—groups that are purposefully and effectively led. When learning about anything, but particularly about other cultures, participating as a group can enable deeper experiences. This longing for something more meaningful can be tapped in groups in ways that are exceptionally difficult to experience on one's own.

> When you ask people about what it is like being part of a great team, what is most striking is the meaningfulness of the experience. People talk about being part of something larger than themselves, of being connected, of being generative. It becomes quite clear that, for many, their experiences as part of truly great teams stand out as singular periods of life lived to the fullest.
>
> (Peter Senge, 2006: 13)

### Adaptive Capacity

The bridge between individual and organizational benefits of 3C, therefore, is leadership.

The study of leadership is inherently interdisciplinary and relies on numerous perspectives to inform the whole. Some disciplines, such as sociology for example, examine power dynamics within and between cultures. Psychology, on the other hand, considers the mind and behavior of the individual. The broad field of leadership incorporates these perspectives and many more. The leader, however, is but one variable in a larger equation. As a practical field of study, leadership considers the environment in which it is practiced as much as the knowledge, skills, abilities and aptitudes required of its practitioners.

If one accepts the future will be characterized by growing levels of volatility, uncertainty, complexity and ambiguity (VUCA), then individuals and organizations capable of adapting to frequently changing environments will be most successful (see De Smet et al., 2021). In immersive experiences involving international travel, each of the four elements of a VUCA environment are typically present.

- **Volatility**: Fast change without a clear predictable trend or pattern.
- **Uncertainty**: Frequently disruptive changes; past is not a predictor of the future.
- **Complexity**: Multiple interdependent causes.
- **Ambiguity**: Little clarity about what is "real" or "true."

Each of these factors requires its own form of critical and creative thinking. But how do individuals put innovation and critical thinking into practice to make organizations better? The answers to this question are made more difficult by interrelated trends that make traditional rules of leadership and management harder to apply (Ibid.: 3).

- *More Connectivity*: free-moving information coming at greater rates because of rising interconnectivity speeds will disrupt rather than facilitate leadership, learning and travel.
- *Lower Transaction Costs*: traditional barriers to entry and costs to achieve scale are disappearing in the economies of the developed world. New businesses will offer competing ways to travel as well as opening rarely experienced locations to a growing number of travelers.
- *Unprecedented Automation*: centuries of management thinking based on mechanization, control, and predictability are becoming obsolete. This factor could homogenize systems and procedures—or the opposite could occur.
- *Fundamental Societal Shifts*: In the developed world, Gen Z and future generations will have fundamentally different expectations about

work and their role within organizations. They will come to expect greater and faster opportunities for promotion, social impact and learning. This will be imported by the developing world and upset traditional social order. (See Zucker et al., 2021.)

Trends like these, among others, amplify the effects of VUCA environments. Yesterday's challenges don't look like today's and tomorrow's challenges are impossible to forecast. Travel experiences to the same country or region will vary year to year. As the rate of cultural change in the developed world has escalated dramatically, so will it eventually change in the developing world. As a result, developing cross-cultural competence will become more challenging over time. Challenges in international travel and engagement with unfamiliar cultures will be magnified by these trends, adding exponentially greater levels of complexity. Unfamiliarity can breed confusion or it can nurture adaptive capacity.

> The critical quality of a leader that determines how that leader will fare in a crucible experience is adaptive capacity. Adaptive capacity allows leaders to respond quickly and intelligently to constant change. It is the ability to identify and seize opportunities. It allows leaders to act and then evaluate results instead of attempting to collect and analyze all the data before acting.
>
> (Warren Bennis)

Experiential development, as we have seen in an earlier chapter, may be the only environment to pursue the quality of adaptive capacity. If immersive experience is the most effective classroom, then the learning organization is the outcome to be achieved in that classroom.

### The Learning Organization

Peter M. Senge, one of the most influential thinkers regarding team function, describes learning organizations as "where people continually expand their capacity to create the results they truly desire, where new and expansive patterns of thinking are nurtured, where collective aspiration is set free, and where people are continually learning to see the whole together" (Senge, 2006: 3). What Senge encourages with this paradigm is learning that enhances the capacity to create. He describes five factors essential for success. All five should be pursued in the development of 3C.

- **Systems Thinking**: Systems theory is the study of concepts and principles that influence how organizations function. Function begins with structure and purpose. How well the organization (or system) adapts to its environment is another. Peter Senge adds to systems theory in a variety of ways, among them an approach to encouraging understanding through "system maps" that depict bounded inter-relationships between organizations (or cultures). Encouraging travelers to "see" inter-relations between and within cultures can be an important first step in true understanding.

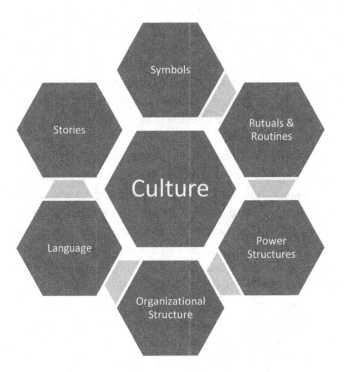

**Figure 8.1** Example of a system map for culture

- **Personal Mastery**: How individuals commit to the process of learning is what Senge refers to as "personal mastery." "People with a high level of personal mastery live in a continual learning mode. They never arrive . . . personal mastery is not something you possess. It is a process. It is a lifelong discipline. People with a high level of personal mastery are acutely aware of their ignorance, their incompetence, their growth areas. And they are deeply self-confident. Paradoxical? Only for those who do not see the journey is the reward" (Senge, 2006: 139). The sheer complexity of 3C demands a high level of personal mastery if it is to be achieved. Continual learning is its hallmark.

- **Mental Models**: We all form theories about the world around us. These theories are formed by "assumptions, generalizations, and images that influence how we understand the world and how we take action" (Ibid.: 8). In a monocultural environment our mental models are ingrained through repetitious exposure. We typically aren't aware of the limitations of our mental models until we've experienced new ones. "The discipline of mental models starts with turning the mirror inward; learning to unearth our internal pictures of the world, to bring them to the surface and hold them rigorously to scrutiny. It also includes the ability to carry on 'learningful' conversations that balance inquiry and advocacy, where people expose their own thinking effectively and make that thinking open to the influence of others" (Ibid.: 9).

- **Shared Vision**: Given the right encouragements, experimentation and innovation can thrive in group settings more effectively than could be done in isolation. When teams, through conversation and debate, develop combinations of ideas, that collective thinking can be more effective if individuals' collaborative inputs are encouraged and respected. When contributors express themselves with clarity and enthusiasm, and leaders reinforce efficient processes, trust is established. "The practice of shared vision involves the skills of unearthing 'shared pictures of the future' that foster genuine commitment and enrollment rather than compliance. In mastering this discipline, leaders learn the counter-productiveness of trying to dictate a vision, no matter how heartfelt" (Ibid.: 9).

- **Team Learning**: A powerful form of learning occurs when the "process of aligning and developing the capacities of a team to create the results its members truly desire" is created (Ibid.: 236). Team learning is the accumulation of individual learning. When people learn in groups, individual's develop more rapidly than they could have on their own.

A traditional approach to leadership, in which the leader dictates outcomes and processes to the led, can be an obstacle to the development of a learning organization. When leading immersive international travel, it is far more efficient to lead in a traditional way by dictating the travel schedule, learning outcomes and all other details of the experience. The primary drawback to any efficiency gained, is the creation of a mindset that resembles a "passive tourist," or someone who simply wants to be told what's important or even interesting. Worse, any rigid or flawed thinking can be transferred to all travelers. Just as the didactic method or "sage on the stage" leads to a suboptimal classroom experience, so too does the "tour guide with all the answers" prevent the synergistic learning available using the learning organization construct.

## TAKEAWAYS FOR THE LEADER IN APPLYING CULTURAL COMPETENCE

Individuals and teams can be led to greater levels of cross-cultural competence through a deliberate developmental program. Key variables within that program are:

- Developing 3C allows for greater cultural adaptability in diverse settings and can lead to an increase in positive psychological outcomes such as optimism, which in turn stimulates a general sense of well-being.
- Focusing on the qualities of empathy and compassion will lead to greater understanding and, ultimately, happiness.
- Visualizing how adaptive capacity can enable 3C in volatile, uncertain, complex and ambiguous environments will lead to more effective travel experiences.
- Incorporating the best practices of learning organizations when traveling in groups will enable everyone to get more from the experience, develop better critical thinking skills and adapt effectively to virtually any environment.

## CULTURAL SELF-ASSESSMENT

1. Why is empathy important to leadership? How can gaining skill in empathetic reasoning make one a better leader?

2. How can compassion be practiced?

3. In what ways can developing 3C lead to better organizational leadership skills and abilities?

## REFERENCES

Bennett, M. J. (1998). *Basic concepts of intercultural communication.* New York, NY: Intercultural Press.

Chen, Y., Su, J., Ren, Z., & Huo, Y. (2019). Optimism and mental health of minority students: Moderating effects of cultural adaptability. *Frontiers in Psychology,* 10, November. Retrieved from www.frontiers.org, accessed August 1, 2021.

Dalai Lama, Desmond Tutu with Abrams Douglass (2016). *The book of joy.* New York, NY: Random House.

De Smet, A., Gagnon, C., & Mygatt, E. (2021). *Organizing for the future: Nine keys to becoming a future-ready company.* McKinsey & Company Organization Practice, January. Retrieved from www.my-mooc.com/en/article/organizing-for-the-future-nine-keys-to-becoming-a-future-ready-company/

Pogosyan, M. (2018). In helping others you help yourself. *Psychology Today.* Retrieved from www.psychologytoday.com/us/blog/between-cultures/201805/in-helping-others-you-help-yourself, accessed August 8, 2021.

Senge, P. M. (2006). *The fifth discipline: The art and practice of the learning organization* (2nd ed.). New York, NY: Penguin Random House.

Sull, D., & Sull, C. (2020). How companies are winning on culture during COVID-19. *MIT Sloan Management Review,* October 28. Retrieved from https://sloanreview.mit.edu/article/how-companies-are-winning-on-culture-during-covid-19/ accessed August 10, 2021.

Wesolowska, K., Hietapakka, L., Eloviainio, M., Aalto, A-M., Kaihlanen, A-M., & Heponiemi, T. (2018). The association between cross-cultural competence and well-being among registered native and foreign-born nurses in Finland. *Plus-one Open Access.* Retrieved from https://journals.plos.org/plosone/article?id=10.1371/journal.pone.0208761, accessed August 1, 2021.

Zucker, R., & Rowell, D. (2021). 6 Strategies for Leading Through Uncertainty. *Harvard Business Review,* April. Retrieved from https://hbr.org/2021/04/6-strategies-for-leading-through-uncertainty

In his foreword to this exceptional book, Dr. Rubenstein began with the most important and oft repeated phrase carried throughout the text, "Leadership matters." Drs. Thomas and Fujimura have provided an even tighter explanation of why leadership matters by knitting together the impacts of cross-cultural competence (3C) as a fundamental competency of truly effective leadership. At this point, unless you skipped to the end, you have digested a wide and diverse collection of research, thoughts and implementation guidelines on leadership and cross-cultural competence (3C). More importantly, you have uncovered a resource that should be on your shelf, at home, on your desk in your office or in your backpack, wherever you are required to perform your responsibilities as a leader. Cross-cultural competent leadership is no longer an option or an afterthought in today's globally connected world, but an absolute requirement.

As a practitioner of leadership for over 45 years and a significant believer in 3C since I was a young military leader, I was engaging the widely varying cultures in the group of young American men I led as well as engaging various cultures in the dynamic Indo-Pacific region. My capstone understanding of the power of 3C integrated leadership came during my service in Iraq over the course of 34 months in various assignments from 2003 to 2010 and was significantly reinforced during my time in the Western Pacific from 2013 to 2015, especially during humanitarian assistance and disaster relief operations in the Philippines and Nepal. From the beginning in the Pacific, through my time as the Commanding General of III Marine Expeditionary Force in Japan, to the end of my career engaging various nations in Europe and Africa, 3C leadership proved the difference between highly successful organizations and those that failed, or at best barely survived. Since leaving military service, my work with professional sports teams, industry and foreign governments has solidified my staunch belief that cross-culturally competent leaders are essential across every profession. *Developing Cross-Cultural Competence for Leaders* provides an excellent set of exercises for leaders at any level to use in any organization, be it military or civilian, in business, sports or academia. As a lifelong practitioner and believer in cross-cultural competent leadership, I have found in this book a single source and detailed resource that can guide every level of leader in their personal development, as well as shaping their teaching, coaching and mentoring of those they lead.

As we focus our National Security posture to great power competition, the need for 3C leaders becomes even more critical than it has been for the past 20 years if that is possible. That is not to say we can forget the tools developed in various regions around the globe over the past 20 years, but the importance of succeeding in multicultural operations around the globe will be driven by cross-culturally competent leaders. Our need for multi-lateral cooperation to defeat nation state adversaries, and our continued need to coordinate with partners and allies around the world to defeat violent extremism, demands 3C leaders. As we continue to lead multicultural organizations in every element of our lives including business, academia and sport, as well as every engagement across the global society, the skills in *Developing Cross-Cultural Competence for Leaders* are vital to our diplomatic, informational, military and economic success. Each of these elements of National Power is truly enhanced by cross-culturally competent leaders at every level of every organization. Relationships are fundamental to success and *Developing Cross-Cultural Competence for Leaders* is the perfect tool for developing those relationships regardless the leader's level in an organization or their education or experience. Perhaps most critical to our nation and our future, the exercises outlined in each chapter will aid immensely in achieving the true power of diversity across every element of our society.

*Developing Cross-Cultural Competence for Leaders* is one of those rare books that is a must reread depending on one's position in life, changing undertaking, or maturation as a leader. Whether leading your peers, leading subordinates or leading those senior to you through your actions and effectiveness, the contents of this book and its combination of research-based facts and refreshingly simple actionable summaries will stand the test of time. Read it with a commitment to understanding and put it into practice in your daily lives. You and those you lead will be better served for your choice to being a cross-culturally competent leader now and well into the future.

Lieutenant General John E. Wissler,
US Marine Corps (Retired)

# Index

Locators in **bold** refer to tables and those in *italics* to figures.

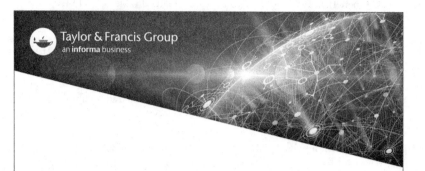

Printed in the United States
by Baker & Taylor Publisher Services